STATE *of* FAITH

God in the Workplace

A survey of spirituality in America's executive suites.

Kirk House Publishers
Minneapolis, Minnesota
and
Mason Smiley Larson, Ltd.
St. Paul, Minnesota

The **STATE** of **FAITH**

God in the Workplace
A survey of spirituality in America's executive suites

Gary Lawrence, Pollster
Rebecca Lunna, Editor
Chris Mikko, Design

Special thanks to all of the sponsoring organizations and all of the executives who participated in the focus groups.

Library of Congress Cataloging-in-Publication data

ISBN 1-886513-90-2

Mason Smiley Larson, 570 Asbury St., Suite 203, St. Paul, MN 55104
Kirk House Publishers, PO Box 390759, Minneapolis, MN 55439
Manufactured in the United States of America

Table of Contents

Introduction

Now, more so than ever before business people want to turn to their places of worship for guidance and support on the issues they confront in the workplace, as well as those relating to their families and communities. It is our responsibility to look out of the church doors, reach out to business people, and work collaboratively to help foster the growth of the entire community. But how can we as pastors, rabbis, priests, and ministers best address the needs of our parishioners?

This is a question that we have frequently asked ourselves at Central Lutheran Church. As a downtown church, we are quite literally positioned between the business and residential communities, and do our best to answer the needs of both.

Often we struggle to find the right context to collaborate with businesses because our worlds are not used to speaking with one another. When it comes to offering guidance about marriage or families, we rarely question what advice we can offer or its relevance that advice to people's lives. When it comes to helping struggling members of our community, we address the issues head-on. While being helpful to the business community can seem a bit more daunting, we shouldn't let it.

We conceived of the State of Faith project to take the temperature of the business community and help us find out what executives are looking for from their churches. We will look to the poll's results to support us as we define what offerings we can provide to executives and corporations.In fact, we have learned a great deal from listening to the executives—both locally and nationwide during the course of this poll. It has shown us that the harvest is plentiful. There are many in the business community who are already focused on issues of spirituality or religion in the workplace, and who regularly make the connection between their work and spiritual lives.

One of the most important things that I learned from the results is that much of what we can provide to the business community is right at our fingertips and well within our skills.

We must listen and learn. Just as we try to connect with the people of our parishes to learn about their personal lives, so must we also learn about their work lives. If we don't know what our parishioners do for work, we need to find out. If we don't know what unique skills each one has to offer, we need to know that too. The better the dialogue between church leadership and business leadership, the better our chances to frame a larger context for our ministries.

Craig Lewis, Senior Pastor
Central Lutheran Church
Minneapolis

Pollster's Note

Contrary to the image many Americans hold of business executives due to highly visible corporate scandals, a recent poll reveals that when one looks beyond Wall Street, U.S. executives as a whole tend to be at least as ethical, religious and spiritual as the average American adult. In some cases they are even more devout in their religious beliefs and expressions. The results come from a survey conducted between May 13 and June 6, 2002, by our firm, Lawrence Research of Santa Ana, Calif. We interviewed a random national sample of 500 business executives, defined as company owners, officers, executives, directors, or managers. The average interview lasted 14 minutes,and the percentages noted in this analysis have a margin of error of 4.2 percentage points.

Prayer in the Workplace

The respondents were told that the topic had to do with what people value and believe, and it was in this context that the business executives were asked early in the interview to imagine they were facing a serious business decision requiring a critical decision. They were asked whether they would do each of five things to help them make that decision. The results:

- Talk it over with a colleague at work — 82 percent
- Pray to God for help or inspiration — 74 percent
- Talk it over with your spouse — 65 percent
- Go off by yourself to meditate — 60 percent
- Talk it over with a spiritual or religious leader — 33 percent

The key point here is that almost as many say they would pray to God for help or inspiration as say they would do what most assume to be the obvious thing to do—that is, talk it over with a work colleague. And more executives say they use prayer more than they do a conversation with a spouse in such a setting. In short, prayer at work is quite commonplace and is used for serious business decisions more often than might be supposed. A later question found that 72 percent claim to have prayed at work by themselves and a substantial 30 percent say they have prayed at work with others.

The disconnect is between the number who pray for inspiration (74 percent) and the number who seek to talk it over with a spiritual or religious leader (33 percent). This indicates that many business executives feel a deep religiosity in their duties and recognize their dependence on a higher power for inspiration, but this devotion does not automatically translate into sharing business problems with a pastor, priest or rabbi.

This reluctance to bring a religious leader into the deliberations is not because execs do not have such a leader to talk to. In fact, 72 percent consider themselves a member of a church or synagogue, so they have had some exposure to a local leader. In addition, 44 percent have had a serious conversation with a pastor, priest, or rabbi leader about theological issues or questions within the last two or three years.

The opportunity for conversation is obviously available. But as noted above, only 33 percent say they would talk over serious business decisions with religious or spiritual leaders, and only 19 percent have actually discussed any type of business problems with them.

So conversations are happening; they're simply happening for less than half of the business community and are not very likely to involve business and career issues. If a business executive sits down with his or her pastor, priest or rabbi, the topic is much more likely to be theological issues or personal, nonbusiness matters such as marital or family problems.

It is total speculation inasmuch as we did not ask a question focused specifically on the reasons why, but perhaps this reticence to open up about business problems lies with the perception that the religious leader may not have had any business experience and, hence, cannot draw from real-life experiences to help the executive. By contrast, most people would recognize that the religious leader has had experience with theology and personal counseling.

Other Religious Practices in the Workplace

In addition to prayer in the workplace, three out of five say they have discussed religion or spiritual concepts with an employee of their company while at work. Though not specifically religious in nature, three-fourths of the executives have counseled an employee or associate at work about their personal problems. These two findings alone go a long way to break the myth of the driven Type A executive who is only concerned about the bottom line.

Another point to note: Three out of 10 keep a Bible or other religious book at work—and half of these people read it at least two or three times a week. These patterns of prayer, scripture reading, and discussions of religious concepts in the workplace are probably well established, as indicated by positions and longevity of the sampled executives. Three out of five of the respondents are owners or business executives of companies with more than 10 employees (this in a country where over 80 percent of all businesses have fewer than 10), and half have been business executives for at least a decade. The point is that it is very unlikely that these religious practices in the workplace only started after 9/11.

Personal Religious Practices

Outside of the workplace, business executives are at least the equal of the average American adult in religious practices and activity. As noted above, 72 percent claim membership in a church or synagogue, while only 64 percent of all Americans claimed such membership in a March 2002 Gallup poll. Aside from weddings and funerals, 42 percent of all Americans attend religious services once a week or more, according to a Pew Trust poll of 2001; among business executives the number is 47 percent. And among those who attend religious services at least a few times a year, the Pew poll says 54 percent of them are "very" or "somewhat involved" in activities at their house of worship; among the same type of business executives in our poll, that number was 58 percent.

What this says is that business executives, perhaps because of their more stable positions and their experience, are more likely than the population as a whole to be religiously active or devout.

Only in prayer patterns does the average American adult outscore business executives. The Pew poll of 2001 measured 59 percent of all Americans saying they pray at least once a day. Among our poll the number was 54 percent.

The business executive also cannot be pigeonholed as a narrow believer, as we found a good amount of tolerance of differing religious beliefs. Fully 80 percent have attended a worship service of a denomination other than their own, and 26 percent have investigated another religion with the possible thought of joining. Though comparable data for all of America is not available, the numbers suggest that the business community is probably more ecumenical and open in nature than Americans as a whole.

In terms of the activities that are recommended and preached by virtually every religion, 88 percent of the business executives have contributed money to charitable groups outside their church, 79 percent have done unpaid volunteer work for charitable groups, and 74 percent have contributed money to their church, synagogue, or religion. Point to note: More have contributed to charitable groups than to their own churches. And in terms of one of the most difficult behaviors to actually perform, 84 percent agree (65 percent strongly agree) with the statement,

"Because of my faith, I have forgiven people who have hurt me deeply." Yes, the statement has a self-congratulatory turn to it and invites a socially acceptable admission. But even discounting it, it still suggests that business execs are probably more forgiving than many have supposed.

The Role of Religion and Spirituality

Fully nine out of 10 business executives consider themselves spiritual, and more than half went beyond that general description and described themselves as religious. The numbers for the three choices presented to the sample for self-assessment were:

- Religious 54 percent
- Spiritual but not religious 36 percent
- Neither 9 percent

In teasing out the role of religious or spiritual beliefs in an executive's life, we asked each respondent to think of major shifts or turning points that have happened in his or her life, and then to describe the role religious or spiritual beliefs played in those turning points:

- Major role 49 percent
- Moderate role 26 percent
- Minor role 14 percent
- No role at all 11 percent

And looking at the role of religion from another angle, both the present poll and Gallup's March 2002 poll measured approximately equal numbers saying that religion is very important in their own lives—58 percent for all adults and 57 percent for business executives.

One other finding confirms the pattern of active religious or spiritual life. Fully two-thirds of the business executives interviewed claimed that they have experienced God's presence or a spiritual force that felt very close to them at least several times; 40 percent said many times, and only 14 percent claimed they have never had such an experience.

Taken together, these spiritual experiences and the recognition of a spiritual or religious influence in their lives at critical junctures confirm that the majority of leaders of America's business community are solidly spiritual people for whom religious beliefs and events have had a major role in forming who they are, a conclusion that obviously contradicts the popular, media-promulgated stereotype of today's business executive.

Ethics

Americans as a whole compared to the business community deviate from one another mainly in their perceptions of business honesty. Five years ago, a *Washington Post/ABC News* poll found that 39 percent of Americans feel that most business executives try to obey the laws governing their profession, while 51 percent said those executives try to find a way around them. Using the same question wording, our poll found that 70 percent of business executives feel their colleagues in business try to obey the laws, and 25 percent said they skirt around them. If the *Post* poll were conducted again today, the people's guess at the number of ethical business executives would undoubtedly be much lower.

The point of interest here is the perception of those who are in the best position to see reality—the business executives themselves. None of them had anything to gain by covering up for colleagues, and the daily headlines about business scandals would have made it easy for the respondents to castigate their community if they had, indeed, observed most executives trying to skirt the laws. As it turned out, fully seven out of 10 believe a majority of executives are ethical. Nonetheless, the cloak isn't completely clean in that a fourth felt most executives try to find a way around the laws governing their profession. And it doesn't take too many of them cutting corners for scandals to build and erupt.

To be sure, the business executives are split when it comes to the battle between smart business and personal ethics. Though the numbers do not necessarily indicate that the business executives themselves would act that way, 46 percent did agree with the statement that "sometimes a business executive has to do the smart business thing regardless of his or her personal ethics," while 52 percent disagreed (38 percent strongly disagreed).

This is a classic case of the glass being half full or half empty. There will be those who will say it is evidence that smart business decisions will come at the price of personal ethics, while others will argue that over half feel that personal ethics need not bow to the corporation. To put this in its proper perspective, we should also point out that 64 percent of the sample disagreed with the statement that "a person committed to his or her religion will have a difficult time competing in today's business world." This finding tends to support those who believe that personal ethics need not be a casualty of the business world, but that an honest businessman or woman can get along and succeed quite nicely while remaining committed to his or her religious principles.

Probing the ethics situation for more detail, we asked the respondents to think of their business competitors and then the people in their own companies. Six out of 10 said their business competitors had done something they consider to be unethical to gain an advantage over them, and 13 percent believed that their competitors have done it to them quite a bit.

As for observations within their own companies, 55 percent said they have seen someone in their company do something that may have been legal but in their view was unethical. The point to note here is that 40 percent said they usually mention it to the offender in such situations, while 12 percent said they usually keep it to themselves. At the very least, it indicates that the vast majority of executives are not shy about speaking up when they see unethical behavior.

Beliefs

When it comes to actual spiritual and religious beliefs, business executives match quite closely the beliefs of the general population of American adults. Drawing from a Gallup 2001 poll of the public at large and using the same question wording, here is the extent to which business executives and all Americans believe in key religious concepts rank, ordered by level of belief:

	Business Executives	All Americans
• Good and evil	96 percent	N/A
• God	91 percent	90 percent
• Sin	89 percent	86 percent
• Heaven	84 percent	83 percent
• Miracles	81 percent	N/A
• Judgment day	80 percent	52 percent
• Hell	71 percent	71 percent
• Life after death	70 percent	70 percent
• The devil	69 percent	68 percent
• Resurrection of the dead	65 percent	65 percent

The only marked difference in the comparison of beliefs is the significantly higher belief held by executives that we will be called to answer to God for our sins on judgment day. Could it be that the business executive, accustomed as he or she is to constant business accountability to higher executives and shareholders, is perhaps more accustomed to and comfortable with the idea of a final accounting with the Supreme Executive?

Gary Lawrence, President
Lawrence Research
Santa Ana, Calif.

Roundtable Discussion

Participants

Jack Fortin is executive director for the Center for Lifelong Learning and the CenteredLife~CenteredWork initiative, a program designed to equip and inspire the people of God for personal vocations and ministry at work, at home, in the community and in congregations. His work at Luther Seminary is a natural extension of the work he has already done to equip the whole people of God to ministry. He began working for Young Life, a non-denominational Christian ministry that works with adolescents, after graduating from Luther Seminary. He saw his positions as area and regional director and then as a divisional vice president as "training and equipping" work. Following Young Life, Fortin worked for World Vision in California and returned to St. Paul to work for Amherst H. Wilder Foundation, directing their experiential education center. Fortin was ordained in 1987.

Curtiss Paul DeYoung is the executive director of the City Gate Project, a Minneapolis organization that develops leaders for ministry in urban multicultural settings. He is also an adjunct assistant professor at Bethel College, where he teaches the course "Martin Luther King Jr., Malcolm X, and our Multicultural World." Prior to his current position, he served for ten years as the president of TURN—Twin Cities Urban Reconciliation Network. Reverend DeYoung has served congregations in Minneapolis; Washington, D.C.; and New York City; and has worked at the Covenant House shelter for homeless and runaway youth in New York City. He is an ordained minister in the Church of God, and is the author of four books on race, religion, and reconciliation.

George Golden is a consulting psychologist, leadership development coach, and adult educator. He has consulted with and developed high potential leaders for 30 years. As Principal of Golden Management Psychologists, he assesses the fit of managers for selection decisions and then helps develop leadership talent. He is an adjunct faculty member in the Executive MBA and MBA programs at the University of St. Thomas's College of Business. He is also a core part-time clinical faculty member at Hamline University's Graduate Programs in Management, and serves as the Associate Director of the Centre for Applied Leadership. A licensed psychologist, Dr. Golden holds a Ph.D. degree from Purdue University and masters degrees in psychology and philosophy.

Gary Lawrence, president, Lawrence Research, Santa Ana, Calif.

Craig Lewis, senior pastor, Central Lutheran Church

Moderator: I am going to open with a question that has come up with interest in every one of our focus groups. It has to do with the challenge that the church faces in the business community. Where is the line drawn between them? Should the church have a position in ethical areas of business, such as Enron? Is that an inappropriate discourse or should it be concerned solely with the spirituality of individuals?

Craig Lewis: No it isn't. I can say, on the one hand I would say that as part of the Evangelical Lutheran Churches of America (ELCA), I sit on the board of corporate responsibility that deals with things like shareholder actions for major corporations etc. On the other hand, our particular calling to the issue is that we also speak to the larger issues to the big business and there are ways in which that does happen. Particularly since the days of South Africa, the church has felt a larger sense of responsibility for our investments and therefore has interacted on ethical issues in a different way with business. If you were to call the ELCA headquarters today and ask does the ELCA have any position with these issues with Enron and others, the church would for the most part try to duck the question. That is certainly true in smaller units—meaning synods and individual congregations. But, on the other hand, we do have statements on economic justice as a denomination, and out of those kinds of statements we frame responses collectively as a church to these issues.

Jack Fortin: I agree with Craig that the church does take positions nationally. But I think it's tough for anyone to be a spokesperson for the church on an issue like Enron. I mean we set ourselves up to fail when we do that. On the other hand, I do think that the congregation is remiss in not being the place where those kinds of things get debated. I also think the church should be a place that people view as a resource in getting a handle on or being able to voice their thoughts. The congregation should be that kind of a place for people, a resource for them in their daily life.

CL: I agree with you wholeheartedly. An example that comes to mind is William Diehl, a business leader who for many years has been trying to help the church understand that we should be pursuing exactly the kind of objective Jack is suggesting.

JF: Yes. Bill and many others from the Lutheran church are really getting very interested in how the congregation can see one of its primary missions as sending people off from Sunday to Monday equipped to talk about these kinds of issues in the workplace.

George Golden: Some other denominations seem to be doing some of this—at least I remember that they were before the events of 9/11. I'm not sure what has transpired since then but prior to that both the Episcopal church—Trinity church—down near Wall Street and one or two of the Jesuit/Catholic parishes down there were starting a lot of this internal dialogue among their members. I am sure they were also offering it to anyone who wanted to come and engage in that type of dialogue. There probably are some "best practices" out there among some churches, albeit very limited.

JF: George, what's your sense in the Jewish community around these kinds of efforts? Historically, the synagogue has been a place where these problems are wrestled with—in many ways much more effectively than in the Christian congregation. Do you have any models in mind there?

GG: I think that you're right but I don't have any explicit models in mind. I would have to do some more factual information gathering.

CL: Last year we had a ministry in the skyways in downtown Minneapolis and out of that ministry, we developed a course in Christian ethics for business leaders. It was remarkably well attended and some corporations, most notably American Express, got so excited about it that they wanted to do additional ones. They gave relief time to executives who wanted to participate in discussions. It was surprisingly successful. One other personal note there, I took the liberty of doing a presentation encouraging business to give us their sense of ethics and how the church should handle its business.

JF: How did that go Craig?

CL: Well, it was a lot of fun. The main thing I was looking for, in my own approach to it was exactly what I got. It was an enthusiastic response from committed Christian business leaders saying, "I never have had a chance to talk about this!"

Moderator: Getting to the individuals, are there particular challenges ministering to business executives as individuals? Is it something that is embraced?

CL: Without really being able to completely answer that question, let me say that one of the issues that I have regularly discovered, has to do with language. Let me use a quick anecdote to explain what I mean. I have a good friend who has a public relations firm. He's always been sort of a nominal Christian, and he joined a conservative church where the Pastor urged him to become a member of the Evangelism committee. My friend came to see me and said, "What on earth is an Evangelism committee?" And I tried to explain it in terms of the business that he's in and he immediately understood and ended up getting very involved in this Evangelism committee. But I use that as an illustration of one of the challenges. A lot of business leaders don't understand the operational words that the church likes to use.

JF: Two different languages.

CL: Exactly that.

Moderator: An interesting point that somebody made in one

of the focus groups that had to do with Enron. And I think that it that it has to do with what you are talking about Craig. He said that he said that he knows some of the executives and that they would consider themselves Christian business executives and more than likely felt that they weren't doing anything unethical or un-Christian. There's a disconnect there somehow isn't there?

GL: When they interviewed Andy Fastow's, the treasurer of Enron, rabbi he said that Fastow was very active and that he was actually surprised he was being targeted so much because the rabbi felt he was one of the more ethical people in the synagogue.

JF: Educator Parker Palmer has been talking a great deal about the difference between the logic of organization and the imperatives of the heart. He is finding in conversations that organizational leaders yearn to pull those two together. Can the congregation be a place that can help support folks who are struggling with those kinds of issues? His point is that the self-preservation logic of organizations or larger institutions or self-preservation really coerces people, I mean that if you don't stay with the imperative of the heart it's easy to get lost. I think for a lot of pastors, I'm speaking as a Lutheran here, that this is foreign territory. It's tough for them to enter into that. I don't know Craig if you would feel that from where you're sitting, but I've talked to so many laypeople in business who say that say as soon as my pastor starts to talk about money, let alone business, they immediately realize that he or she doesn't have any idea what it's like to deal with goods and services. They really want to have that conversation, but don't know where to have it.

CL: I very much agree with you, Jack. Also, since you mentioned Parker Palmer, I have been very interested in what he has to say about these kinds of issues. One of the things you have to say both to the church and I think to business leadership is that you need to understand the difference between the internal ethical dimension and the external ethical dimensions of the work you do. Part of what you're saying there is you know both pastors and business leaders have a leadership in terms of how you influence others. But what's happening in terms of how you are influencing your own thinking—are you in touch with your own heart?

GL: Another interesting point from the survey is a situation that we posed. Let's say you're facing a serious business situation like a critical decision that effects your business. Only 33 percent said they would talk that kind of decision over with a spiritual or religious leader. Now 72 percent of these are people who belong to a church or a synagogue and that compares with 64 percent of all American adults. So these were people who were above average in being a member of a church or synagogue and yet only 33 percent said they would talk over a serious business situation about a critical decision with a spiritual or religious leader.

JF: Yes. That matches the work that Laura Nash has done at Harvard and in the book she wrote with Scotty McLennan, *Church on Sunday Work on Monday: A Guide to Reflection.* She says that there is this growing yearning to pull more of ourselves together in the workplace. There are 1500 web sites out there now on spirituality in the workplace with a corresponding lack of interest of going to the congregation—whether it's Jewish, Christian or whatever for help. Instead, she says from her reviews—this is why I'm so interested in what you all found out—that people are making it up. They are saying, "What I need is a balanced life. I've got to get things in balance, I have to survive in this world. I am going to eat blueberries and granola for nutrition and I'm going to do yoga, I'm going to go to the church for maybe the sacrament". They put together a compilation of things and are still finding themselves somewhat empty, but don't know where to turn. Their journey continues without stopping to look at the traditional structures for help. So, what does that say about our structures? But what you're saying would certainly follow suit. If there is a difficult decision, if that pathway is not paved back to some congregational, faith-centered community for support. They are going other places.

GL: Seventy-five percent of these people agree and say that their faith is involved in every aspect of their lives. So we are not dealing with a business community that's non-faithful.

JF: Yes. Perhaps just disinterested.

CL: Let me use an example that has taken place in the last week. One of our members is a former ELCA pastor of 15 years ago who is a successful stockbroker today at a big firm and he has been crying the blues about this down cycle for some time. When I saw what happened to the market the day before yesterday, I said you know I really ought to talk to Jim and I didn't. Jim wanted to talk to me and I wanted to talk to Jim and yet, we hadn't spoken with one another.

CD: I find it interesting in your poll that the respondents say that faith impacts every decision they make, yet when they go to make a decision they don't appeal to any of their spiritual leaders. That seems to be a contradiction of the way that they are defining faith. It does make me wonder if there still isn't a disconnect. I mean, if they had a concern around marketing, they would go to an expert on marketing, but when it comes to ethical questions they don't seem to be inviting in people who can speak to that perspective, which may be how you can be an Enron executive that goes to church to hear a good sermon on Sunday and then make decisions that seem to be contradictory to that throughout the week. The other side of that, I think that often pastors are somewhat intimidated by business executives, or they are often afraid to speak to them because they are often some of the largest donors and givers to their congregation. I think there is that challenge as well to play that sort of prophetic or spiritual role in the lives of executives.

GL: A follow up on that, the additional questions that we asked, asking them to looked back over the last two or three years on any conversation they have had with any religious leaders only 19 percent said that they have had such a discussion with a religious leader over business problems, but 44 percent claim they have had the discussion with a religious leader over theological issues or questions, and one-third of them said that they have had such a discussion over personal, marital, or family problems. So I interpret that to say that there is a connection, a fairly good connection, with their religious leaders, such as they have had something beyond a social conversation with a pastor, priest, or rabbi about theological issues, personal issues or family or marital problems, so the connection is there should one or the other decide to bring up business problems. It's just that for some of them it is off limits even though for so many other things within their lives it's within the limits.

JF: I think that's indicative of the issues. Our sense of the congregation's mission has too long been programs inside the church, which often deal with the personal and the family. We are better at that than wrestling with the work place and yet, I would define work as one of the places where we are vested. I'm not talking about only that part of your work you get paid for, because single moms have a workplace as well. What I want to know is how do we bring the workplace and the issues where people spend between 40,000 to 100,000 of their life, an area that is somehow disconnected, into the church? If we look at the prayers of the church, many churches usually only pray for people out of work or who have died or are sick, but we don't pray about the people at work, the auditors or the accountants around April 15th, or the people working fifty hours a week at Christmastime. We don't tend to pray for the people who are actually doing the work. It's a big challenge to say that in a world in which the Christian church is no longer the empire church, a world of many religions and culture around us now that we are living in a world of many cultures and many religions in which our focus has to be applied to our communities in sending our people out from Sunday to Monday equipped to respond and live faithfully in a very diverse world. I think that is a new challenge for the church and I think it's one of the reasons that many of our congregations are dying. They don't give that kind of vitality to their members.

CL: I certainly agree with that statement and several others that were made before. Let me say to you Gary that the statistics that you just read are sort of born out by my experiences as a parish pastor with business executives in the congregation. I wanted to pick up a comment that Curtiss made. One of the great hymns of the church that we all sing is 'Tiptoe through the tithers'—it seems that is what we do when it comes to business and faith.

And also, there is a statement that was once attributed to the Democratic party that I think can be attributed to the church many times: The church loves jobs, but hates employers.

Moderator: If a business person has a problem marketing a product, they'll go to a marketer. And according to our poll, about three-fourths of them would pray to God for help or inspiration. Only about one-third of them would talk over a critical business decision with a spiritual or religious leader. Is that perhaps a shortcoming of the churches?

CL: Would it be fair to say that there is some implicit evaluation going on there?

CD: What does that say about the way we are equipping the future leadership of the church, the pastors and other leaders? Are we allowing them to intern in places of work, not just in places of faith—in communities of work, not just communities of faith, so that they do get a more comfortable sense of that.

GL: I am just wondering how many business executives feel that their pastor or religious leader knows my daily routine or has been there and has run a small business before. I just put it out on the table as a curiosity item. I am wondering whether they don't make that leap to talking about business problems because they wonder if the pastor has any similar backgrounds in which he can refer.

JF: I would agree with that.

CD: This is a shift, I think, in the church moving into the urban environment or to the metro environment. I think during the days when we were more agrarian or rural focused, the pastor used to visit the farmer and understood the farm and understood that area of life. It does seem as though our life has grown more complex, that it is more difficult for the pastor to understand. And being a seminary-trained person, I know our seminaries are not helping us with understanding. We hardly learn how to do a budget for our church, let alone learn what it takes to run a company. There is certainly a gap in the training for our pastors in how to engage with folks that are out in the marketplace, which is the majority of the membership.

JF: We have successfully weaned away even those pastors in the rural areas that go to the farms. They're now trying to build programs and compete with their urban and suburban counterparts, mistakenly thinking that a large church is somehow successful, instead of trying to meet the needs and really be relevant to the people in their daily lives.

GL: Just as they have take your daughter to work day they should have take your pastor to work day.

JF: You know, Craig, you have a very unique past and it seems to me, with its combination of business acumen and financial background, that you are uniquely placed to call the church leadership to a greater awareness of how we might enter more meaningfully into the daily life of our parishioners. You've had that experience and people know it. How do you reflect on that when you are with your fellow pastors? Do you feel that you are speaking out of a different environment?

CL: Well, first, thank you for raising that. Yes, I feel that absolutely and I'm out there doing a little evangelizing on that issue. One of the ways that I start is that I say to other pastors, for example, "Yes, I have been involved in not-for-profit management for 30 years, I have been in economic development for many years, but I had to go to for-profit business before it occurred to me that a free market economy is not a bad way to distribute goods and services. That's my way of trying to say that many of my colleagues in the ministry, we don't even get the basic economics.

GG: In teaching about this and working with executives for some thirty years as a consultant and adult educator, my sense is that the dialogue is insufferably poor between the two groups, between business people and congregational leaders. There is also very little applied theology of work, of spirituality at work, and of leadership. And since neither side knows much about what the other means, but they are both scared of dialogue, I don't find it very surprising that many people aren't taking the initiative to start talking. It's scary.

JF: George, you have invited me to sit in and speak to your course [on faith in the workplace] at St. Thomas. I have found however, and I wonder if it is true with the other clergy types that you bring in, that the conversation is incredible and they are marked by a lot of surprise.

GG: Total surprise. Surprise that people are really thinking about and dealing with and looking for these kinds of resources. And that is the trouble. It doesn't exist in too many places. It's difficult to pull together, to even offer guide pins—I say pins because many of the resources are not thick enough to be posts yet. I think that's part of the dilemma: the churches offer a lot of theology about work and ideal states, and spirituality and ideal states, and leadership for those in positions of power, but those are insufficient for the 21st century. Therefore, to get back to your comment earlier, people are picking it up on the fly because they don't see it too many other places. They have to find another executive who's willing to dialogue about it. There are many executives who get together and discuss this and there are also people who are starting to dialogue at other levels in the organization. But they don't have many guidelines or models.

JF: Craig, what if Luther Seminary and Central and others teamed up and developed an institute of business engagement or something, where we take advantage of your leadership as a senior pastor, but we'd also begin to use the resources here. We have more to learn and it would be an opportunity to engage with people of the church.

GG: You might want to make it ecumenical too. I think that there are other religious groups in town that would run real quickly across town to do it with you.

JF: I think, George, that you would be a good one to help us with that. It could be very interesting to have a few people come together particularly around the congregation and to make it okay for people to begin talking about this.

CL: One quick thing that I have thought about in respect to that. I have wondered about, and am aware of, a number of Christian conversations that take place among business leaders in boardrooms. I don't know if a congregational base or locations can afford the same opportunity as what I see going on right now to whatever degree it happens.

JF: Well, maybe part of what we're doing is encouraging conversations in the workplace and not so much within the congregation. We want to talk about how to support and encourage those kinds of informal conversations at critical times, especially if we don't define the church as a building, but as God's people who work in the world.

CL: I certainly agree. One of the things that I have learned in doing this asset based mapping is that it's helpful to start with knowing the places where it has already taken place.

GL: Along with that point in the questionnaire, you saw how many spiritual or religious items were actually done in the workplace. Fifty-nine percent claimed that they have discussed religion or spiritual concepts with an employee of their company at the workplace, 72 percent have prayed at work by themselves, 30 percent have prayed at work with others. Now, there's a major one. And so it tells me that if you start something that sends a signal, that some people are discussing business ethics or business concepts with their pastor, and I think it would spread quite quickly.

JF: One of the nuances that we haven't addressed is this: We have a lot of groups that are in or around the parish or the congregation that are gathering or supporting business in a variety of ways. But I'm concerned that very few of these groups are dealing with both the person and the person's organization. I see a lot of support groups for individuals coping with an institution that they somehow think is neutral and has no character but is simply there to either be manipulated or coped with. I think that there is a real need by business people, as I'm listening to them, to be in a group that helps that business person strategically think about their impact on their organization. Who else in their organization can they identify as people who want to hold and trust the larger values of that organization. In other words, we have small groups that help people cope, but we don't have small groups that help people strategize and that then support them for their efforts in the workplace. It's all about the one and the many—not just supporting the individual. We don't have a good sense of organizational callings, organizational vocations, I think that's a whole arena that needs to be addressed.

GG: I couldn't agree more. I think that's where the issues I was talking about before—work, leadership, and then spirituality in the workplace—are located: within that organizational calling.

JF: Curtiss, I wanted to ask you a question about your work in urban communities. In some of the congregations that I have had in the urban core, particularly African American congregations, it seems like there is a more natural sense of bringing your daily life back into the congregation because the congregation serves as more than just a spiritual place. It's often the place where social movements and change in the community gets addressed or at least talked through. What kind of phenomena are we dealing with here?

CD: I think that's an excellent point that you make Jack and I think that there may be some cultural or sociological perspective. I mean, what we've been talking about as a challenge earlier, how does one integrate their faith into their business life, and their business life into their church. You know for some, those things are just separate, it's their sort of belief system, but that's not always the case within other cultures, particularly among African American congregations. I think you'd find it perhaps in the Hmong and Latino communities here as well, that business start-ups and those are supported by church folks. Church folks may be some of your first customers. The church is a part of your network for developing a business. I think Alfred Babington-Johnson's Stairstep Initiative is one of the best examples of that sort of bridge between church and business within the African American community and I think that it's always been sort of a holistic view. It's very Old Testament or more of a Hebrew Scripture perspective where Israel just saw everything—economy, government, and so on—were all sort of integrated and we certainly see that as true. It does seem to be not apparent in the suburban settings.

JF: I was just wondering if there were models. I mean it would be wonderful if we could find models in the urban core from which we could get some learning and some best practices and a way to look at this as a more holistic way of viewing the congregational support and life.

CL: There are a couple of examples I don't know if this would be quite the same as the ones you and Curtiss are discussing but a guy like Kirby Caldwell, coming out of the business community became a leader and began to integrate business leadership with the leadership of his own congregation where to do the remarkable development Windsor Villagem and there are a few others around the country that are starting to do that. That would be one of the directions that I'd look at for best practice.

Moderator: One of the things that we found in the poll is that 53 percent of the respondents considered themselves religious and 36 percent considered themselves spiritual but not religious. What does that mean? What are the ramifications of that and does it surprise you?

JF: For some people, I think the term religious connotes a certain religious behavior. The fear of proselytizing or wearing your beliefs on your sleeves so to speak, as opposed to spiritual where a person might be saying, "I don't want to be a religious person but that doesn't mean that I don't have a spiritual core, that I don't pray, that I don't see that there is meaning and hope outside myself, or that I can't draw on a God that's loving and present in my life". I see that too with the Gallup poll, which found that people don't normally want to talk about religion or talk about living a religious life, but they do want to talk about the notion of spirituality.

CL: It's very interesting—there would be a lot of people who, starting with Wade Clark Ruth, and others who have done studies of generations would say that phenomena is much generational as much as anything else.

JF: Is that right? How so?

CL: That there are many people who understand really entirely the kind of taxonomy or systems they need to understand and which generation is which.

But I feel safe to say that those 30 and under are far more inclined to describe themselves as spiritual but not religious and so the age of the responder may be as important than anything. There have been some pretty decent monographs that have been written about the spiritual but not religious category. In fact, right now it is considered a significant category.

JF: In 1999, Gallup asked if people felt the need for spiritual growth and 78 percent of the business community said yes. In 1994 when he asked that question only 20 percent of the business community said yes. I found that quite remarkable because there is a 58 percent swing in people's interest but it sure matches what Lauren Ash found out.

GF: I think that definitely there is a generation emphasis here, but I have also talked to many people 50 and over as well, and many of them I think are burned out by their religious experience or view it as just dogmatic or beliefs and/or they don't see the connection to the workplace. Some of them have said that in their view they have moved beyond what religion has to offer them for day-to-day sustenance. So, I don't think that it's just generational. I think that there's a whole bunch of different subgroups within that spiritual but not religious category.

CD: Just on the spiritual versus the religious, I do think that many people are disappointed with the institutions of religion—it could be the TV evangelists, it could be their local congregation and certainly where you see a lot of fallout from the current issues in the Catholic Church around sexual abuse that many people will remain 'spiritual' but will be so disappointed in their religious institutions that they will back away from considering themselves religious. And for a minute, going back to just one thing from your original question about why hasn't there been any public statement from the religious community from Enron.

I think that again, it is much about how we've defined our faith, in the conversation that we've had thus far we've said that the church and the synagogue and the mosque are really good in dealing with the family and the personal and the interpersonal and so you hear religious institutions speak out against these kinds of issues. They have positions on abortion, homosexuality, or other kinds of things that are family related. But because there has been such a disconnect within the work place and the business community when something like Enron happens and there's this pause where everyone is sort of waiting for the moral voice of the community to speak out, there is no word. So I think if we rectify some of the other pieces and there's a better integration, then there would be more public statements on those issues.

JF: I entirely concur with that.

GL: In terms of how the business community themselves view things, I'll call your attention to that one question that where we ask people, "Would you say the most business executives try to obey the laws that govern their profession, or try to find their way around the laws, among the business community?", 70 percent say business executives try to obey the law, when that same question was posed a few years ago by the *Washington Post/ABC News* poll, they got 39 percent of all Americans felt that business executives try to obey the law. That number is probably down a little bit, but with what happened with Enron, Anderson, Tyco, and then, World Com restating their earnings and all that kind of thing. Among the business community themselves, they try to obey the laws, that's pretty good.

JF: Of course, there is a major difference between intent and behavior. They want to obey the law, but what about all of the pressures that keep it from it.

GF: I have a question on that issue. On question number forty-six. Will the business executive do the smart business thing regardless of his personal ethics? Forty-six percent said yes. The next question says, "My faith is involved in every aspect?" Seventy-two percent. There's a disconnect.

GL: And they're compartmentalizing their attitudes.

CL: One last kind of anecdote that may or may not be useful to this conversation, my last day in banking I had an exit interview, more of a friendly thing with the chairman of the board of the bank. As we talked through, he made a confession, which I knew several years before hand that he had been a Jesuit candidate for the priesthood and that he was so turned off by the priesthood, that he decided to go into business instead. I told him that I had felt exactly the same way and that was why I decided to pursue being a pastor.

Chapter 2

Questionnaire and Topline Results

Hello, may I please speak with [name on sample list]? This is [caller name]. I'm with Lawrence Research, a national research firm. We're conducting a national public opinion poll with business owners and executives. The topic of our study is what people value and believe, and many of our questions are the same as the Gallup Poll. May I interview you? It will only take about 11 or 12 minutes.

Question

First of all, how many employees are there in your company, counting yourself?

Minneapolis/St. Paul

• 4 to 10	27
• 11 to 25	17
• 26 to 100	19
• 101 to 250	5
• More than 250	32

National

- 4 to 10 — 41
- 11 to 25 — 21
- 26 to 100 — 15
- 101 to 250 — 6
- More than 250 — 16
- No Opinion — 2

Question

And how long have you been an owner or an executive in a business?

Minneapolis/St. Paul

- Less than 5 years — 33
- 5 years up to 10 years — 20
- 10 years up to 15 — 19
- 15 years up to 25 — 16
- 25 years or more — 12

National

- Less than 5 years — 29
- 5 years up to 10 years — 21
- 10 years up to 15 — 14
- 15 years up to 25 — 19
- 25 years or more — 17
- No Opinion/Refused — *

Question

Sometimes when we look around us, we wish that our society had more of a particular value, or that people had more of a certain characteristic. When you think of all of the traits and values that we in America need more of, what one value do you feel is missing the most?

Question

As a business executive, you have to make decisions. Let's say you are facing a serious business situation and must make a critical decision that affects your business. For each item I read, please tell me whether it is something you would or would not do in such a situation.

Minneapolis/St. Paul

	Would	Would Not	No Opinion/Refused
• Talk it over with a colleague at work	90	9	2
• Talk it over with your spouse	68	28	3
• Talk it over with a spiritual or religious leader	24	73	4
• Pray to God for help or inspiration	66	34	1
• Go off by yourself to meditate	52	47	*

National

	Would	Would Not	No Opinion/Refused
• Talk it over with a colleague at work	82	15	3
• Talk it over with your spouse	65	30	5
• Talk it over with a spiritual or religious leader	33	63	4
• Pray to God for help or inspiration	74	25	1
• Go off by yourself to meditate	61	39	*

Question

[Split Sample 1:]
Let's say you need to hire someone in your sales department. For the sake of the example, two men apply for the job, Mr. A and Mr. B. If the following descriptions were all you knew about each one, which one would you probably hire?

> Mr. A graduated from a top university with an A-minus average. He is single, well dressed, and articulate. He worked his way through college in a fast-food restaurant.
>
> Mr. B graduated from a state college with a B average. He is newly married, looks nice, and is soft spoken. He worked during the summers in his father's business.

Minneapolis/St. Paul

• Would hire Mr. A	40
• Would hire Mr. B	40
• No opinion	20

National

• Would hire Mr. A	34
• Would hire Mr. B	49
• No opinion	17

Question

[Split Sample 2:]
Let's say you need to hire someone in your sales department. For the sake of the example, two men apply for the job, Mr. A and Mr. B. If the following descriptions were all you knew about each one, which one would you probably hire?

> Mr. A graduated from a top university with an A minus average. He is single, well dressed and articulate. He

worked his way through college in a fast-food restaurant. He mentioned he's not particularly religious.

Mr. B graduated from a state college with a B average. He is newly married, looks nice and is soft spoken. He worked during the summers in his father's business. He mentioned he attends church every week.

Minneapolis/St. Paul

• Would hire Mr. A	39
• Would hire Mr. B	37
• No opinion	24

National

• Would hire Mr. A	27
• Would hire Mr. B	51
• No opinion	22

Question

[Everybody]
Just your best guess. Would you say that most business executives try to obey the laws governing their profession, or would you say most business executives try to find a way around the laws governing their profession?

Minneapolis/St. Paul

• Try to obey the laws	74
• Try to find way around laws	23
• No opinion	3

National

• Try to obey the laws	70
• Try to find way around laws	25
• No opinion	6

Question

Have your business competitors ever done something you consider to be unethical to gain an advantage over you? IF YES, ASK: Does that happen quite a bit, occasionally, or not very often?

Minneapolis/St. Paul

• Yes/Quite a bit	12
• Yes/Occasionally	28
• Yes/Not very often	21
• Yes/No opinion	1
• No	37
• No Opinion/Refused	1

National

• Yes / Quite a bit	13
• Yes / Occasionally	27
• Yes / Not very often	18
• Yes / No Opinion	1
• No	40
• No Opinion/Refused	2

Question

Have you ever seen someone in your company do something that may have been legal, but in your view was unethical? (IF YES, ASK:) In such situations, do you usually mention it to them or just keep quiet about it?

Minneapolis/St. Paul

• Yes/Usually mention	47
• Yes/Usually keep quiet	10
• Yes/No Opinion	4
• No	38
• Refused	1

National

• Yes/Usually mention	40
• Yes/Usually keep quiet	12
• Yes/No Opinion	3
• No	43
• Refused	2

Question

As we go through life, there are from time to time major shifts or turning points in the direction we are going. Some we choose and others are imposed on us by outside events. As you think about these events in your life, what role did your religious or spiritual beliefs play: a major role, a moderate role, a minor role, or no role at all in helping you through these points?

Minneapolis/St. Paul

• Major role	39
• Moderate role	32
• Minor role	18
• No role at all	10
• No Opinion	1

National

• Major role	49
• Moderate role	26
• Minor role	14
• No role at all	11
• No Opinion	1

Question

Which of the following statements comes closest to describing your beliefs: you are religious, you are spiritual but not religious, or you are neither?

Minneapolis/St. Paul

• Religious	49
• Spiritual but not religious	41
• Neither	8
• No Opinion	2

National

• Religious	53
• Spiritual but not religious	36
• Neither	9
• No Opinion	2

Question

Think back over the last two or three years and the conversations that you may have had with any religious leaders. Not counting social conversations, have you had a serious conversation within the last two or three years with a pastor, priest, or rabbi about: (READ IN RANDOM ORDER)

Minneapolis/St. Paul

Yes	No	Refused
• Theological issues or questions		
45	55	*
• Personal, marital or family problems		
29	71	*
• Business problems		
14	86	*
• Career or employment decisions		
14	85	*

National

Yes	No	Refused
• Theological issues or questions		
44	55	1

• Personal, marital or family problems

33 66 *

• Business problems

19 81 *

• Career or employment decisions

17 83 *

Question

Have you ever:

Minneapolis/St. Paul

Yes	No	Refused
• Prayed at work by yourself?		
66	34	*
• Prayed at work with others?		
20	80	*
• Counseled an employee or associate at work about their personal problems?		
84	16	*
• Discussed religion or spiritual concepts with any employee of your company at your work place?		
51	48	1
• Discussed religion or spiritual concepts with any employee of your company outside of your work place?		
50	49	1
• Attended a worship service of any denomination other than your own?		
87	13	0
• Investigated another religion with the possible thought of joining?		
28	72	0

National

	Yes	No	Refused
• Prayed at work by yourself?	72	27	*
• Prayed at work with others?	30	69	1
• Counseled an employee or associate at work about their personal problems?	76	24	1
• Discussed religion or spiritual concepts with any employee of your company at your work place?	59	40	1
• Discussed religion or spiritual concepts with any employee of your company outside of your work place?	55	45	*
• Attended a worship service of any denomination other than your own?	81	19	1
• Investigated another religion with the possible thought of joining?	26	74	0

Question

Do you keep a Bible or any other religious book at work? IF YES, ASK: How often do you read in it during breaks or lunch time: daily, two or three times a week, weekly, two or three times a month, monthly, or less frequently than that?

Minneapolis/St. Paul

• Yes/daily	4
• Yes/2-3 times a week	5
• Yes/weekly	4
• Yes/2-3 times a month	1
• Yes/monthly	4

• Yes/less frequently than monthly	6
• Yes/No Opinion/Refused	1
• No/No Bible or religious book at work	76
• Refused	0

National

• Yes/daily	9
• Yes/2-3 times a week	7
• Yes/weekly	3
• Yes/2-3 times a month	2
• Yes/monthly	2
• Yes/less frequently than monthly	7
• Yes/No Opinion/Refused	2
• No, no Bible or religious book at work	69
• Refused	0

Question

Are you a member of a church or synagogue?

Minneapolis/St. Paul

• Yes	75
• No	25
• Refused	0

National

• Yes	72
• No	28
• Refused	*

Question

Aside from weddings and funerals, how often do you attend religious services: more than once a week, once a week, once or twice a month, a few times a year, seldom, or never?

Minneapolis/St. Paul

• More than once a week	7
• Once a week	38
• Once or twice a month	23
• A few times a year	17
• Seldom	12
• Never	4
• No Opinion/Refused	0

National

• More than once a week	16
• Once a week	31
• Once or twice a month	17
• A few times a year	15
• Seldom	15
• Never	6
• No Opinion/Refused	*

Question

If attends church at least a few times a year, ask: (N=251)

Aside from attending religious services, how involved are you in activities at your church or house of worship? Would you say you are: very involved, somewhat involved, not too involved, or not at all involved?

Minneapolis/St. Paul

• Very involved	17
• Somewhat involved	35
• Not too involved	27
• Not at all involved	21
• No Opinion/Refused	0

National

- Very involved 27
- Somewhat involved 32
- Not too involved 22
- Not at all involved 20
- No Opinion/Refused *

Question

People practice their religions in different ways. Outside of attending religious services, do you pray: several times a day, once a day, a few times a week, once a week or less, or never?

Minneapolis/St. Paul

- Several times a day 26
- Once a day 22
- A few times a week 21
- Once a week or less 22
- Never 9
- No Opinion/Refused 1

National

- Several times a day 36
- Once a day 18
- A few times a week 18
- Once a week or less 16
- Never 10
- No Opinion/Refused 1

Question

How important would you say religion is in your own life: very important, fairly important, or not very important at all?

Minneapolis/St. Paul

- Very important 53

- Fairly important 31
- Not very important at all 16
- No Opinion 1

National

- Very important 57
- Fairly important 26
- Not very important at all 17
- No Opinion 1

Question

For each of the following items I am going to read you, please tell me whether it is: something you believe in, something you're not sure about, or something you do not believe in.

Minneapolis/St. Paul

Believe	Not sure	Don't believe	No opinion
• God			
91	6	3	*
• The devil			
64	14	21	1
• Heaven			
81	11	8	*
• Hell			
62	17	21	*
• Miracles			
81	11	8	*
• Life after death			
71	19	10	1
• Sin			
91	3	5	1
• Resurrection of the dead			
60	19	21	1
• Good and evil			
97	2	1	*

National

Believe	Not sure	Don't believe	No opinion
• God			
92	5	3	1
• The devil			
69	11	19	1
• Heaven			
84	8	7	*
• Hell			
71	11	17	*
• Miracles			
81	10	9	*
• Life after death			
70	17	12	1
• Sin			
89	4	5	2
• Resurrection of the dead			
65	15	20	1
• Good and evil			
96	2	1	1

Question

How often would you say you have experienced God's presence or a spiritual force that felt very close to you: many times, several times, once or twice, or never?

Minneapolis/St. Paul

• Many times	34
• Several times	23
• Once or twice	29
• Never	13
• No Opinion	1

National

• Many times	40
• Several times	26
• Once or twice	19
• Never	14
• No Opinion	3

Question

I will now read you some statements. For each one, please tell me whether you: strongly agree, somewhat agree, somewhat disagree or strongly disagree.

Minneapolis/St. Paul

Strongly Agree	Somewhat Agree	Somewhat Disagree	Strongly Disagree	No Opinion
• A person committed to his or her religion will have a difficult time competing in today's business world.				
4	12	23	58	3
• Sometimes a business executive has to do the smart business thing regardless of his or her personal ethics.				
21	25	15	37	2
• My faith is involved in every aspect of my life.				
33	39	13	13	1
• We will all be called before God at the judgment day to answer for our sins.				
54	22	7	12	6
• Because of my faith, I have forgiven people who have hurt me deeply.				
53	29	7	9	2

National

Strongly Agree	Somewhat Agree	Somewhat Disagree	Strongly Disagree	No Opinion
• A person committed to his or her religion will have a difficult time competing in today's business world.				
10	14	21	53	3

• Sometimes a business executive has to do the smart business thing regardless of his or her personal ethics.

22	24	14	37	3

• My faith is involved in every aspect of my life.

47	28	12	11	2

• We will all be called before God at the judgment day to answer for our sins.

68	12	6	9	5

• Because of my faith, I have forgiven people who have hurt me deeply.

65	19	6	6	4

Question

Within the last 12 months, have you:

Minneapolis/St. Paul

Yes	No	Refused
• Done any unpaid volunteer work for any charitable organizations or groups that help people?		
84	16	0
• Contributed money to any charitable organization or other group, not including your church?		
94	6	0
• Contributed money to your church, synagogue or religion?		
81	18	1

National

Yes	No	Refused
• Done any unpaid volunteer work for any charitable organizations or groups that help people?		
79	21	*
• Contributed money to any charitable organization or other group, not including your church?		
88	11	1

• Contributed money to your church, synagogue or religion?

74	25	1

Question

Were you raised in any particular religious denomination? (IF YES:) Which one?

Minneapolis/St. Paul

• Assembly of God	1
• Baptist	5
• Buddhist	*
• Catholic	35
• Christian Science	*
• Church of Christ	2
• Church of God	0
• Disciples of Christ	0
• Episcopal	*
• Greek Orthodox	*
• Hindu	*
• Islam/Muslim	0
• Jehovah's Witness	*
• Jewish	1
• LDS/Mormon	*
• Lutheran	31
• Methodist	5
• Pentecostal	1
• Presbyterian	4
• Quaker	0
• Russian Orthodox	0
• Seventh Day Adventist	0
• Shinto	0
• Unitarian/Universalist	*
• Non-Denominational Christian	1
• Other	2

No	7
Refused	3

National

• Assembly of God	*
• Baptist	15
• Buddhist	*
• Catholic	26
• Christian Science	1
• Church of Christ	2
• Church of God	*
• Disciples of Christ	*
• Episcopal	2
• Greek Orthodox	*
• Hindu	0
• Islam / Muslim	0
• Jehovah's Witness	*
• Jewish	3
• LDS / Mormon	3
• Lutheran	8
• Methodist	11
• Pentecostal	2
• Presbyterian	7
• Quaker	*
• Russian Orthodox	0
• Seventh Day Adventist	1
• Shinto	0
• Unitarian/Universalist	1
• Non-Denominational Christian	4
• Other	1
No	9
Refused	3

Question

Do you consider yourself to be part of any particular religious denomination today? (IF YES:) Which one? (IF NO:) Do you consider yourself to be atheist, agnostic, or you just don't have a religious preference?

Minneapolis/St. Paul

Yes:

• Assembly of God	1
• Baptist	3
• Buddhist	*
• Catholic	28
• Christian Science	*
• Church of Christ	1
• Church of God	0
• Disciples of Christ	*
• Episcopal	1
• Greek Orthodox	0
• Hindu	*
• Islam/Muslim	0
• Jehovah's Witness	0
• Jewish	2
• LDS/Mormon	*
• Lutheran	24
• Methodist	3
• Pentecostal	0
• Presbyterian	1
• Quaker	*
• Russian Orthodox	0
• Seventh Day Adventist	0
• Shinto	0
• Unitarian/Universalist	1
• Non-Denominational Christian	5
• Other	1

No:

• Agnostic	3
• Atheist	0
• No religious preference	19

Refused: 4

National

Yes:

• Assembly of God	*
• Baptist	9
• Buddhist	*
• Catholic	18
• Christian Science	1
• Church of Christ	2
• Church of God	*
• Disciples of Christ	1
• Episcopal	2
• Greek Orthodox	0
• Hindu	0
• Islam / Muslim	0
• Jehovah's Witness	*
• Jewish	3
• LDS / Mormon	4
• Lutheran	5
• Methodist	6
• Pentecostal	2
• Presbyterian	6
• Quaker	0
• Russian Orthodox	0
• Seventh Day Adventist	*
• Shinto	0
• Unitarian/Universalist	1

• Non-Denominational Christian	6
Other	2
No:	
• Agnostic	4
• Atheist	1
• No religious preference	21

Refused 6

Question

IF CHRISTIAN, ASK: (N=210)
Would you describe yourself as a "born-again" or evangelical Christian, or not?

Minneapolis/St. Paul

• Yes	30
• No	67
• Refused	3

National

• Yes	43
• No	51
• Refused	6

And a few final questions for statistical purposes.

Question

What is the last year of school you have completed?

Minneapolis/St. Paul

• Less than high school	1
• High school graduate	9
• Some college/vocational	26

• College graduate	47
• Post-graduate degree	16
• Refused	1

National

• Less than high school	3
• High school graduate	17
• Some college/vocational	30
• College graduate	31
• Post-graduate degree	18
• Refused	1

Question

Which of these statements best describes how conservative or liberal you are? (ROTATE READING TOP-TO-BOTTOM OR VICE-VERSA)

Minneapolis/St. Paul

• Very conservative	14
• Somewhat conservative	33
• Neither conserv nor liberal	18
• Somewhat liberal	25
• Very liberal	9
• Refused	1

National

• Very conservative	20
• Somewhat conservative	37
• Neither conserv nor liberal	17
• Somewhat liberal	18
• Very liberal	6
• Refused	3

Question

What is your age, please?

Minneapolis/St. Paul

• 18-24	1
• 25-34	13
• 35-44	27
• 45-54	28
• 55-64	20
• 65 +	9
• Refused	1

National

• 18-24	2
• 25-34	15
• 35-44	23
• 45-54	23
• 55-64	21
• 65 +	13
• Refused	2

Question

Are you currently registered to vote? (IF YES:) Are you registered as, or consider yourself to be, a Republican, a Democrat, or something else?

Minneapolis/St. Paul

• Yes/Republican	38
• Yes/Democrat	13
• Yes/Independent/Other	37
• Yes/Refused	7
• No, not registered	5

National

- Yes/ Republican 47
- Yes/ Democrat 24
- Yes/ Independent/Other 21
- Yes/ Refused 3
- No, not registered 6

Question

What is your Zip code?

Question

Sex

Minneapolis/St. Paul

- Male 59
- Female 41

National

- Male 58
- Female 42

Question

Post code: state code

Question

Post code: phone number

That completes our interview. Thank you for talking with us today.

Chapter 3

Focus Group A

Here is an open-ended question. It came right out of the poll, and I want to get your response to it. I will read it in verbatim: "Sometimes when we look around us, we wish that our society had more of a particular value, or that people had more of a certain characteristic. When you think of all of the traits and values that we in America need more of, what one value do you feel is missing the most?"

- Integrity comes to mind.
- Integrity.
- Moral compass. Direction.
- Honesty.
- Trust and integrity.

Let's say you were facing a situation where you had to make a decision that would affect your business. I am going to read some things and just say what comes into your mind more as an explanation than as an answer. For each item, tell me whether this is something that you would or would not do: A) talk it over with a colleague at work, B) talk it over with your spouse, C) talk it over with a spiritual or religious leader, D) pray for help or inspiration, or E) go off by yourself. Which one

sounds like something you would do, and why?

• Well, I would talk with a colleague if one were available because that's my nature. I would talk with my wife when she asks, "How was your day?"

• I hate to say that that's exactly what I was going to say, but it's pretty darn close. I would talk to my wife or spouse if she brought it up.

What about the spiritual aspect of business? Are there times when you talk about business decisions based on spirituality or religion or something that would be seen as a nontraditional part of business decision-making?

• If you are trying to make a decision about something that involves ethics, or about how to handle a people problem, then that's when that might come into play. But if the question is something like, "Should I expand?" or "Should I buy a machine?", then that's probably not going to come into play.

• It depends on who you are talking to. If the customer or whoever you are talking to is a spiritual person, then you can bring that up. But I think a lot of people feel uncomfortable bringing that up in conversation, and you don't want to try and test them. You don't want to say the wrong thing.

Would you say that business leaders—business executives—obey the rules, the laws of a profession? Or would you say that the game of running a business is to see how closely you can get around the rules?

• From my standpoint, it's very much black and white. There are rules, there are certain things that I operate under—especially in the financial world—that have become much greater and much more extensive in how I work my way around an issue or ethical piece to find a back door. And it definitely puts you on the space alone. Many people—especially in Enron and those other cases—are focused on how to avoid taxation, how to avoid a given rule or guideline. The idea is to find a way around it, and then write another guideline and find your way around it. I see that as an ongoing battle both in business and government.

How much of spirituality—your own personal spirituality—drives how you look at those things?

• I think each individual is probably different, but personally, that drives it extensively. Part of how I am trying to serve the Lord is through my actions in the workplace.

• In what I observe, there's a great deal of it when there's personal accountability for a decision. But when it's a decision that's made somewhat anonymously, more often than not it's:"What does the culture allow?" That standard appears to be a lot lower. Or: "What can you get away with?"

• I'm going to dump the pot into two different areas, and then back up. The first one is how well do you want to sleep at night and feel comfortable morally and consciously, versus what is your objective financially? Very often those two conflict in a big way. So you've got financial implications as well as moral implications, and they tear a decision into very opposite directions. The second point is that a lot of it is in how you were raised and your basic sense of right and wrong. The [sense of] right and wrong that I grew up with, or the mores that society created are there regardless of your level of spirituality. And so we've got different issues here. I don't necessarily say, "Gee, I better pray and decide," when I'm confronted with the question of whether something is right or wrong. I've got a benchmark that I was taught which drives where that line is drawn.

Are there things that happen in your companies that would be legal but which you might consider unethical? Perhaps some of your colleagues or some of the people over whom you have management control—but who don't share your ethics—will look at a situation and say, "I think we should do this." Would that happen?

• I think it depends entirely on what kind of people you have. Most of the people I work with have the same values I do, so we don't have that routinely come up.

How did that happen? How did you emerge with a corporate culture of shared values?

• First of all, we're tiny. We have about seven or 10 employees and we didn't run any ads to get people. It's all been kind of referral-based and church-based, so we ended up with people who all think about the same. I find that sometimes when there is a conflict, I'll be the most conscious of the ethics involved. Not because I'm better or worse, but just because that's the way I see things. Other people might be more interested in the profit as one of the things. I might be less interested in that.

Does anyone have a deal that they have changed because it seemed unethical?

• I come from a larger corporation and there's a lot of weasels in our business—and in our competition. You know them the minute they come through the door; you just know there are things that are going on behind there. But it's a financial decision that they make to get ahead, and they know that eventually someday it's going to catch up with them. But they go ahead and make those decisions every day to try and get ahead financially. When you get into that end of the business, sometimes you get almost caught up in it because of the corporate dollars that they need and the dollars that they ask for on a monthly basis or a quarterly basis to keep their targets and keep their shareholders happy. So do you get to that point where you know you can unethically make money by saying the wrong thing, or do you just say, "I'm not going to go there"? It's a daily part of our business.

• I think it varies industry to industry. I think some industries are inherently more unethical or have the opportunity to be more unethical. We've all gotten the calls from the guy in New York City selling stock.

• Eventually it's going to catch up with them. They might reap the benefits for a couple of months, but it's going to catch up to them.

In your business, if the goal is more financial than exclusively ethical, does it drop the ethical standards of the whole industry?

• Yes. In my industry—the printing industry—there's so much competition in the market these days that people are doing things that they normally wouldn't do.

As you see the economy start to slow down, do you see more fast and loose sales?

• I'm not going to define it as fast and loose, I would simply say the need—and I think you said the stress—that people are under is greater.

• Users have gotten more creative in what they ask for, or any kind of information that they share that they normally didn't share could drive prices down and get the better deal because they are under stress and they are making those capital decisions and they are getting the best deal. How can they do that? For us it's both sides—first, how creative can we get, and how creative is the end-user getting, and when do you say we're not going to do one of those parameters because it's getting too creative? You know, I think that's a tough call to make when you are searching for business and you have to say, "You know, I'd rather walk away from this deal because it goes against my beliefs or ethics."

Does it make it more difficult to be an ethical business person?

• I see executives accepting the unethical behavior of others even though they didn't do it and positioning themselves to benefit from it.

• I would argue economically that it's a little bit different, that you go back in the late 1800s and early 1920s and it is very much the same. I think that you have cultural mores or cycles. You go from the Victorian to a very liberal background. We are probably moving the curve back to the other side from the 1960s, 1970s, and 1980s. I'm not sure if we brought the business guys in from 1910-1918 that you couldn't get the same discussions that you're getting with Enron.

Let me tell you the following question's results from the poll. The question was, "Which of the following statements comes closest to describing your beliefs: Religious, spiritual but not religious, or neither?" Fifty-three percent of the executives said they were religious, 36 percent said they were spiritual but not religious, and 9 percent said neither. What's your take on

that question?

• I would ask what's their definition of religious and spiritual.

• Yeah, I mean what does that really mean? I think everyone's definition of that is different.

Does the number of those executives say that they are neither surprise you? Is that a high number or a low number?

• I think that it is both.

• Given the emphasis on separation of church and state, which eventually leads to the separation of church from anything, I am surprised that's not happening more.

• I think that there's a certain trendiness in being spiritual, but not religious—you know, where you worship the earth or define your own religion or something.

• I would say also that a good chunk would say that they are religious, but they are not evangelical.

In your experience, how much religion or spirituality is evident in the workplace? Do you think it's more evident than it used to be, less evident, or not at all?

• It was very evident after 9/11. There were more people willing to talk about it.

What about with Enron and the new focus on what the newspapers would call holding the corporation's feet to the fire of ethics?

• I haven't heard those conversations turn spiritual. I might have heard them turn to integrity or turn to ethics, but I don't recall any of those conversations turning spiritual.

• Actually, the people I know—and I know some of the players at Enron—absolutely acting what they thought was the appropriate legal sense to the tax code. I don't think in their minds, that they saw the fallout being this dramatic, for one, and two, I think they felt like the decision they were making was not a religious right-or-wrong decision. It was a financial, tax-angle decision.

• What about how they cashed in though just before all of this hit. And made hundreds of millions of dollars?

• That's a good question.

• But the guys you know probably didn't do that.

• No, actually some of them did.

• So much of the Internet boom changed the dynamics for corporate America. They were watching guys who started a business and were working for six months and would suddenly be worth millions of dollars. And they are going you know, we have this billion dollar revenue business and why am I only getting paid this? And that whole sense of entitlement just shot off of the charts. So when they did it, did they do it thinking that I am just going to sneak away? [Maybe] they almost felt they were entitled to it because the Yahoo guy or the guy who started America Online and some of them they make these huge [amounts of money] and I am not sure their wealth is any more honest than Enron's.

Is there a cautionary tale in Enron that has effects in your

own business that has to do with ethics and spirituality?

• Just don't get that big.

• I still wonder if at the time they thought they were doing the wrong thing? If they had it to do again given the same circumstances, would they do the same thing?

• I think the answer to that is no.

• None of them in my mind ever believed that the company would go bankrupt. You are asking about religion and workplace and as far as talking about going to church, talking about going to a wedding, or if I'm going my nephew's baptism I think that those conversations are very active and people are aware of religion at work and the impact of it is there. But as for speaking directly to God's influence on business on a day-to-day basis, I think that it's very tight, very different.

• If one of my coworkers comes at religion from a different direction than I'm at, it doesn't make either of us right or wrong. Our relationship with God might be different, but I'd say I'm private about it.

Do you think people who would talk about their religion at work are more ethical than those who wouldn't? Is there a connection between being committed to your faith and being more ethical in the workplace?

• No. Not always.

• Just because he is more private doesn't mean he is any less ethical because I am more outspoken to people at work about it.

• I think that growing up in Oklahoma impacted the way I see it. Oral Roberts and his family had a huge religious impact in that area. You know little old ladies were sending checks from Mississippi every month, so I would say just the opposite. But that's biased.

• I think a lot of times, especially where I work, you could be considered a Bible-thumper or kind of looked down at. If anybody would come around in my office where there are 300 to 400 people to discuss religion you can probably consider that you'd be bothering somebody.

• And I think it raises the question in people's minds: Am I being leveraged, or what do you want from me, this is my personal space, why are you coming into my personal space, is there an angle here? And then everybody's guard goes up.

• I think people are looking for hypocrisy. If somebody says something about their faith, then immediately people are going to watch them to be able to ask: "Is this guy true to what he is saying, or is this just his shtick?"

• Religious groups are a wonderful way to network. You can go into some of these core groups with or without these beliefs and create a very big network almost immediately, so you almost have to be sure that you're not just getting networked.

In your business experiences does the Bible ever come up in everyday conversations? Or does God come up in business decision-making?

• Not as much as it should.

How should it?

• Well, I probably think about it more than I say it. Maybe that's good, maybe that's bad, but there are probably times when I'm making decisions that I am trying to figure out what God would want me to do. But I am not telling people that is my thought process so they are not involved in it that way even though I work with people who would be interested in that.

• I think it depends on where you work. And it's different everywhere. Plus there are a wide variety of people that work in one place and that have all different kinds of beliefs.

• I would argue that it's been pretty much forced out. Certainly in the last 15 to 20 years there's diversity issues, and diversity training and a lot of the politically correct discussion. How do you bring up the Bible where you may have Jewish people, Muslims, and Christians all mixed in the same room?

• The people who I have seen having success, bringing the talk of the Bible or God into the workplace didn't lead with it. First and foremost they were good at business—it's about numbers. Now I'll tell you why. The guy who leads with good numbers and good business and all of that, does he have an opportunity as a man of faith to share? Yeah, I think he does, but he didn't lead with it. There are, right or wrong, those who lead with it before there is an established business capability and it's almost like, put up with my lesser end on the business side because I am leading with this. God is not a guarantee of good business. People claiming they are religious are not automatically good business people.

• In my mind it is more of a voice and sense of an inner core and it is very hard to be public with it.

• Human resources people usually say just don't talk about it. They say don't even bring it up and it's the easy way out. It's part of sexual discrimination and everything. This is what you don't talk about or you could get into trouble. Or you could get reprimanded, or somebody could actually say they don't like that and report you to human resources, and you might have a problem down the road so just don't bring these specific subjects up.

• How is that for our First Amendment right though? I am just curious, in a court of law, how would that stand?

• Inside a corporation I don't think that it matters.

• They don't say that you can't do that, but they do say that this is what you could avoid.

We're going to shift gears a little bit. I'd like you to comment on a couple of statements. I'll read just a few of them and tell me if you agree or disagree. A person committed to his or her religion will have a difficult time competing in today's business world.

• Disagree.

• Disagree.

• Because I think that's probably one of your biggest assets, depending on how you do it. If you have that kind of foundation, typically you'll have a strong work ethic.

• I think it goes back to the first question you asked about what value we all value, and that was integrity. I think that most people out in the marketplace are looking for that same value, they are looking for somebody they can count on when the chips are down. Are they going to do the right thing? It's like when something goes wrong, that's when they test to see what you are really like.

Let's say your nephew is applying for a job and asks, "Should I talk about my personal relationship with Jesus Christ in my job interview?" What do you tell him?

- No.

- I would say no.

- I would say no because it has no relevance to the job.

- It's a bonus because maybe those who believe in Jesus Christ could produce integrity more often than those who don't. But what you are interested primarily in is business success. If you are looking for integrity then go for integrity, but I don't necessarily consider Christians the group that I go after for integrity. You go after the business ability first and integrity second, and if they happen to be people of faith, that's a bonus.

- Male, female, gay, straight, religious or not, or whatever—it shouldn't make a difference.

Let's look at it in a different way. Someone is applying for a job with you and goes out of his or her way to tell you that he or she is a Christian. As a manager, how do you see that?

- I would be watching to see if other stuff they say seems to add up with that statement.

- You know, I'm going to be the odd man out here and say yes. If you've got to advertise it, to some degree something is missing.

How would you expect an employee to feel about you if you wore your faith on your sleeve during an interview or during a business relationship? Should a manager advertise his or her faith?

- If they ask, yes, I don't see why not. If they asked questions I would answer them, but I wouldn't just go right out and say, "Yeah, I'm a believer, how about you?"

Chapter 4

Focus Group B

For the first question, I'll read one that comes right from the poll. "Sometimes when we look around us, we wish that our society had more of a particular value, or that people had more of a certain characteristic. When you think of all of the traits and values that we in America need more of, what one value do you feel is missing the most?

- Honesty.

- Responsibility.

- Accountability.

- Yeah, that's the word I was going to say.

- I think the number one lacking thing is humility.

- I think there is lack of charity.

How so?

• I think that people of my generation—I'm 43—are still locked in the 1980s. They are chasing the buck and everything else, even their own children, has to take a back seat. I think that charity begins at home.

What about the issue of accountability? Do you feel like it is a collective responsibility, or the responsibility of others to keep people in check, or is it personal accountability?

• I think it's individual. People should feel that way and then everybody suffers because people feel that way. But I think it's really on the individual person. For whatever reason we've got to act like we're not supposed to care about others, and we're not supposed to be honest with others, share with others, be concerned about others; it's all about me or my company and whatever is necessary for us to get ahead.

Are there other industries that you would look at and immediately say are lacking?

• Well, I think this whole Arthur Andersen thing and the values there are just absolutely incomprehensible. I mean everybody talked about the 1980s and 1990s, but that was nothing compared to how much apparently went on at the highest levels of corporate America. The lack of integrity, honesty, accountability, the hollow values. Anything goes, we can hide this or hide that and construct this. Corporate America is just incomprehensible. So to me it is the whole values and what we really stand for, and basically it is not very much. Then you have tens of thousands of people losing their money as a result of the Enron situation. And nobody seems to care. I can't figure that out. No one is concerned about the people who are going broke.

• Yeah. We're talking $743 million. You've got people who have lost their entire retirement and you don't think there is something wrong with that? I mean not wrong with the fact [that the people who ran Enron] cheated, but wrong with the fact that they basically might as well be highwaymen—they might as well mug people on the street.

Do you think that there is more of this kind of corporate behavior to come? And that our shock value is decreasing and we get desensitized to that kind of news?

• I think there is more to come, but I think that it's the end of that kind of cycle because it's catching up with a lot of people from that whole 1990s bubble—the dot-coms and that sort of thing, but there is still some cleansing. I think that it will result in some changes.

And what about that 1990s dot-com bubble?

• I think it was an attitude. I think that the attitudes change. I think that was the quick way of making a buck. I don't think the attitude has changed, I don't know what's out there now, but there's got to be a game out there that people are looking at and saying, "OK, now we can make a ton of money doing this quickly." The attitude hasn't changed.

• I think the dot-coms are really just part of a larger picture. Everyone was riding the stock market and that thing was going to hit 20,000. This is beautiful, protect the bottom line, and whatever it takes to make that happen and people don't matter. We have to go to the board meeting, we have to look at the stockholders and we have to make them happy. And it's just going to go forever. There is some perverse pleasure in watching what is happening in the market.

• What I can't get—and it might just be me—is how you can look somebody in the eye [and rip them off]. People at some of these companies knowingly ripped off their employees. They knew they were going to go under. I don't understand it. Employees came in and the people were saying, "They shut down and you have a half hour to get out." It is the most mind-boggling thing. When the [bosses of these sorts of companies] say, "I hired you into an honest corporation," they basically con you. That attitude is not gone. Are we morally bankrupt? I mean there are 3,000 people dead in New York City because some people covered their butts—whether or not they were or were not doing their job. Does it get much worse than that?

Do you feel that there is an ebb of flow to that kind of behavior? For example, the 1980s and 1990s were a time when you saw an increase of moral bankruptcy or unethical behavior, and do you think we will come back from that and have a readjustment in our attitudes?

• We've had a shift in the last four years. Yeah it will swing back and forth, we're looking for revival.

• It's about the winners. Winning is money. That's what gets people, you know. That's what got them to say, "OK, it's about winning." It means that those are the winners, and unfortunately we don't look at the honest businesses and winners anymore. We don't look at sports athletes as winners, it's all about money. Whoever makes the most money is the winner. That's the unfortunate part.

What about the people who came of age in the 1980s and 1990s do they have the moral resources that are needed to conduct themselves ethically in today's business world?

• I think in the post 9/11 world we have an opportunity for goodness to come forth from people. [But now it seems that] the country already wants to move on. I had some hope at first because you saw things of faith become important overnight, but I think churchgoing numbers have gone back to where they were

9/10. When the next attack comes, we'll see what happens. I don't know if they learned enough ethically in school during 1980s and 1990s. You couldn't go to a bar at night without talking about how you were going to make your millions, at least in the early 1980s. I didn't learn anything ethically during my school time.

Where can that generation turn to find resources when they have questions about ethics in the workplace—or where would you suggest people get that?

• Church is obviously the biggest place—or it should be. I don't know if we are really a society that values that, but I think that it is almost on a shame level to believe in God. There used to be a time in America when everything was sort of ended as that way. People really meant it because that was part of how they were raised, and it was part of their lifestyle. If you don't have that until you are an adult I don't know where you get that from. It might be 9/11. I know that they had more applications to be firefighters than ever in history [immediately after 9/11] because people saw them as heroes. That says something, but I don't know where that other faith comes from, or that other belief system comes from if you don't have it in your initial childhood or young adulthood.

Let's talk about hiring practices. Let's say you were hiring someone in your business and they went out of their way to make a point that they were religious or that they were a frequent attendee of church. Would that be positive or negative or nothing?

• For me, I tend to overspiritualize everything because I believe in God and truth. I think that if somebody says they are religious, we're hardwired to seek things that are spiritual and there is an awful lot on the table right now that's spiritual, but a lot of it is pretty empty and a lot of damage has been done. Christians have done—if you are looking from a Judeo-Christian worldview—a lot of damage. They are the ones thumping people over the head with the Bible saying, "This is the way you are going to heaven and this is the way you are going to hell." So, I am sort of indifferent if somebody tells me that they are religious because I wouldn't know what that meant. There has to be some flexibility to have a conversation about what that means. Generally, I would say that is positive because at least it is somebody who is saying that there is something bigger and more important than me out there and I guess that's a good first step.

- They are willing to take a blow because that is definitely a will take one for that attitude. They will they lose more opportunities than they will get, and that means that they are willing to take it.

What would you do if you have a situation that you are confronted with in your business and you need to make a critical decision and it's got an ethical basis? I am going to read a couple of things and I want to know what your reaction would be—and if it is something you would or would not do in a certain situation. Would you talk the decision over with a colleague a work?

- Possibly.

- Yes.

Would you talk it over with your spouse?

- Yes.

- Yes.

• Yes.

Would you talk it over with a spiritual or religious leader?

• Possibly.

• Perhaps.

• Perhaps.

What would prevent you from taking that ethical situation to a spiritual or religious leader?

• I think that there is a real separation in our society between church and state. There is a real world and there is a spiritual world. I think we don't use them together. Again, that's part of this whole separation thing that we have gone through in the last several decades between how we were initially raised. I think that the church has become less involved in our day-to-day activity. I just don't know if it's even real world any more.

• We are also trying to reidentify who those spiritual leaders are to us.

• I was going to say it's the old: Where have you gone Joe Dimaggio? Who are the heroes? I look at my church right here and right now, and my church is in the headlines every day because we've got some bad apples somewhere. So who do you go talk to? Who do you trust? Thinking back to the comment about the real world and the spiritual world, where I live, the spiritual world is the real world, but we've made that comparable. It's systemic. There are four years of a real shift in the way we think about life. If you go back and look at the movies that were made

40 or 50 years ago God was very preferable. He's not now.

• It isn't in the attitude of it, the way people talk. It was in the way people made the projects. There was a belief-of-faith system in films and television. It was accepted. Now if it's there it's all spent out. We have lost something, and it has been gradual over the years and it has been subtle.

I am going to read a couple of additional statements and then for each one please tell me if you strongly agree, agree, disagree, or strongly disagree. First, a person committed to his/her religion will have a difficult time competing in today's business world.

• I argue on both sides of that one.

• I am going to say I agree.

Why?

• If you are a religious person, you are bound by certain moral conditions and you can walk a certain walk if you are truly following what your religion is telling you. But if you're not, anything goes. So in a competition, the playing field is not level. That's the I-agree point. Now, the reverse side of that: If I am truly religious and I am a spiritual person, I would pray for additional help, so that's where it isn't.

• And also, if you believe that you are not in competition, you will not have to compete. The right way to pull yourself out of it is that it's not your journey and that's the way it's supposed to be. If they make $100 million, then they are supposed to make $100 million. That's their place, it's not yours just because you're a believer. In the basic process, people will do what ever is necessary. It's all about the Benjamins. Once you think that way, you can't win because you are concerned about what will happen to the people who will. Again, the guys at Enron are fine—they have nice houses, their kids get to go to the best grade schools, and they have great vacation homes. But what about the 65-year-old couple [who lost] all of their retirement and they are now working at McDonald's, and are trying to keep their house. They didn't send them a check and say, "Here let me pay your house payment."

Sometimes a business executive has to do the smart business thing regardless of his/her personal ethics. Do you strongly agree, agree, disagree, or strongly disagree?

- I disagree.

- I disagree.

- I strongly disagree.

Do you think that you are among the majority or the minority?

- Minority.

- At the risk of judging my brethren? (Laughter)

- I agree.

My faith is involved in every aspect of my life, including my business decisions? Strongly agree, agree, disagree, and strongly disagree?

- Strongly agree.

• Disagree.

Just your best guess. Would you say that executives try to obey the laws governing their profession, or would you say that most business executives try to find a way around the laws governing their profession?

• Yeah. I think most try to follow the rules in regards to what profession they are in. I don't know if that's just me wanting to believe. I basically believe most people are good.

• I feel like I see a lot of both.

• I think that most people are basically good. I think that it's interesting that the ones who make it to the top are maybe the ones who weren't on the level playing field that we're talking about here.

• Maybe it's just that the bad stick out more than the good.

• That's another difficult question to answer. It's how you see the world. Take the guys from Enron—I wouldn't want to be around them. I want to go to people who are really the right people.

• It makes it harder to make a case for acting ethically in a business where there's unethical behavior going on.

• A perfect example is when you are with the cops, especially the undercover cops. Everybody lies all of the time and then you lie. You have to because everybody is lying, so pretty soon nothing is real. Nothing is real except what comes out of your mouth at that moment. Everything you're telling them is not real, what you're telling them is not real. So if the reality is shifted, then you have a change of reality to an environment where there are people who are good and people who you like, and then it becomes different.

Have your business competitors ever done something that you would consider to be unethical to gain an advantage over you?

- Yeah. Nobody in this room can say that's not true.

To what extent is it unethical?

- The changes of it. The ethics of it have become kind of murky. They are going to do whatever is necessary, but that is who they are. You can say, "I would never do that," but they're going to do that and you know that they are going to do that. So you work your advantages based on the fact. That is their approach to this. I'm going to do it my way on what I believe is honest because I [want to create] a better product or [have] more attentiveness or better service. Then I am going to try to get an account based on that or maintain the account based on that. Because what they are going to do is lie and cheat and cut the corners and go under the table.

Is it at all shocking to you that the answer would be: Of course—of course somebody has done something unethical?

- No.

Does that discourage you?

- No. You have a finite amount of time on this planet and you can take the high road or not. I chose to do that, for better or for worse. I'm not discouraged. I think people will come around eventually. I'm an optimist. There are signs of hope on the horizon now. I think there are 30-somethings out there right now who are really spiritually hungry, and who are looking to do the right thing. [The question is] if we at the 40- and 50-year-old level can follow their example. I see some real hope in it.

• I think that if you don't have faith you will be discouraged because then there is no hope and you feel like you've been abused and misused. I think when you have faith you basically have to accept the fact that faith is the answer. You can't be discouraged, because that's why you've got faith. That's what it is really all about. There is always going to be that group of people.

Have you ever seen someone in your work experience do something that might not have been legal, but in your view was unethical?

• Yeah.

• Yeah.

If you have, in that kind of situation do you bring it to their attention or do you keep quiet about it?

• I think that you should at least let people know what you believe. I don't think it is a fight. I just think it is a matter of saying, "We should do this, or I think that's wrong." I just think you've got to say, "It's wrong and I don't want to be part of it." And that's just an individual choice. Whether the company goes forward with it or not, I don't want to be part of it.

• It is so much more about what you do opposed to what you say. In the particular case that you take to task, I don't know. It depends how close it gets to you or the people you know. You don't do it because it's wrong. Hopefully it changes someone else's life over time.

• I am a Christian. I think that you have to show by example. If you are going around and yelling at [people] that's not going to change them. All they are going to do is get angry at you and the situation, and they will probably just end up doing it. I think that you are supposed to lead by example and that means that you look at them and say, "No, I don't want to do that."

Chapter 5

Focus Group C

Sometimes when we look around us we wish our society had more of a particular value or that people had more of a certain characteristic. When you think about all of the traits and values that we in America need more of, what one value do you find that we are missing the most and why?

• Concern for the common good over individual concerns.

• Trust. And being able to trust our government leaders, our teachers, our school superintendents—all of those people who make decisions. Business people. Politicians.

• I think my answer is rooted in trust itself. It has to do with not assuming that ignorance does automatically lead to hate and crime and that, instead, it has to do with lack of understanding. Any kind of intolerance is usually based on a failure to understand a cultural difference or other differences.

I am going to read a few items aloud. Tell me whether or not this is something you would do if you were facing a business situation where you had to make a morally or ethically based decision. Would you go home and talk it over with your spouse or significant other?

• (All individually) Yes.

Would you talk it over with a colleague at work?

• Perhaps.

• Sure.

• The caveat that I would add for both of those questions is that it would also depend on whether or not it was a part of my function not to or at that particular person's request that I not. So if I was asked specifically not to share it with my spouse or another colleague then I would want to be careful how I proceed. Other than that I would say yes to both as well.

• Some decisions are so clear that you don't have to talk to anybody about it. So the ones that you end up talking about are those that you are really asking if they are or aren't the right decision. There are a lot of decisions that are right and a lot of them that are wrong, and then there are some in the middle that you just don't know. But I think that there are relatively few of those compared to the others.

Would you discuss the situation with a faith leader, whether it's a rabbi, priest, minister, etc.?

• Less likely.

• I would say no.

Why not?

• I have a couple of very good friends who are members of the clergy so if I did speak to them, I would be approaching them because I was friends with them not because they were members of the clergy.

• I think in the scenario that you mapped out, trying to get them up to speed on the context in which this dilemma occurred feels like too big of a hurdle. Our spouses and our significant others are involved enough in our daily lives so that we can bring them up to speed quickly and they can understand the context of how we feel in this position. But if I went to my senior pastor and said that I have a thing going on with work, I would spend the first 45 minutes talking about where I work and what I do since I'm not sure my pastor even knows what I do. Trying to create the context about what happened would be too time-consuming.

• Yeah, I was going to say that I would have really thought of that in the first place. It seems contextually out of place.

• It seems out of place. I would agree.

• I do hold certain values for my faith, but I don't turn to my faith leader for moral dilemmas of any aspect in my life. Not just for work, it's true elsewhere as well.

• I'll turn the tables because I don't have a faith that I subscribe to so I wouldn't have anyone to go to.

Let's talk about the issue of accountability in a corporation or a business? Who's responsibility do you feel like it is to be an ethical watchdog in a corporate environment? Is it your responsibility to keep others in check if they aren't doing it themselves?

• You know, I really admire the people like Sherron Watkins for what she did to stand up and say there's something not right here. I know that you can be in a really difficult spot—it's a lot to have to ask. I think that we do have that obligation to be honest but my gosh, when your job is at risk that's a hard cross to bear.

• Generally speaking, I would say to the best of our abilities absolutely. It's a collective responsibility, but it's made up of all of the individuals.

• Some of that responsibility we tend to associate with the supervisory capacity. That's where it gets down to the company's formal structure, and it really depends a lot upon the skills and abilities of that person. But as a whole, I think we have collective responsibility when it comes to ethical decisions. But I agree it's a tough row to hoe.

• I think the whole culture of Silicon Valley is just a scary development for our nation. I worked for a Silicon Valley company before I came here and there was a noticeable difference in how they looked at laws. I'd be the first one to say that there is a little bit of a gray area in a law. I think it would be OK to push the boundaries a little bit, depending on the situation, but there was a culture in Silicon Valley that was more like, "Law-shmaw—we are the golden children and we will do whatever we have to do to make this thing public. You saw just a whole new level, I think, of disregard for common rules or common standards.

If actions speak louder than words, then what do the actions of the upper management at places like Enron and WorldCom say about today's business environment and ethical behavior?

• The overarching thing it says is there's a disregard for the common good and I think that's severely lacking, and I think it speaks to trust and it speaks to loyalty and all of those sorts of things. I think that is says that everybody is about themselves.

• What's interesting to me is the way the markets respond to this. The stock market is in a terrible place because individual investors are afraid their investments are not safely placed. Then they sit with an investment that can go from $50 to 20 cents over a couple of months because of the actions of a handful of folks. I actually like that response because it means that the money still is talking. All of those larger companies need those investment positions and what they're going to find is that actions by a handful of people who have gone under the table will get seen and when they do, the stock gets obliterated and that's unacceptable. I think it will cause a new set of standards to be enacted because they can't afford to have the stock price targeted that way.

• I feel the same way about the dot-com-bomb thing. To me, it is the same way of speaking back and saying, "enough is enough," and this is how people respond to that.

• They were being hugely rewarded financially too. I think that what we're seeing now is that things happen on a pendulum, and we're finding that we're reaping the benefit or tribulation of that mentality with all of the things that we've seen in the news lately. But I don't know that we have reached the pendulum peak, or if there's yet more to go before we swing back.

• The part that I'm bitter about is that the upper-level people made millions of dollars and people like me lost from my stinky little stocks in my 401(K) like everybody else.

• I think it's about greed. What forces greed, in some respects, is personal security. I think that people are feeling less personal security today than they ever have. We don't see the people who work at 3M for 30 years anymore like we used to. Back then it was a given.

You talked about the pendulum. Do you think that some of this is generational—that the next generation of business leaders is less faithful, less ethical, or had an upbringing that is not as rooted in religion?

• I don't think so.

• I don't think so either. I think it has more to do with the fact that so much of what we do is about ourselves that we lose track of the people beside us. I can't care about others if I don't know them and understand them. So, it's not about me being taught to care. It's that I don't have the benefit of knowing a person well enough to get the feelings that go along with that. It's a silly example in some ways, but we talk about road rage. You sit inside a car as though you are the only one on the road, and everything else is an obstacle. Those aren't other people 6 feet away, they're an obstacle to where I want to go. With the way we use technology and the way we manage our time, there is so little free time to get to know other people. We have narrowed that down to a little box that's only about me, and I just don't care about anybody around me, so I don't see them. But it's not because I was taught not to care.

• We talk a lot about—particularly in my organization—the value of community and what technology can do to help foster that, particularly in greater Minnesota. Whether it's a physical community or it's a faith-based community, I think those points are well taken that it's about time to reconnect.

• The irony is that a lot of this is coming from the people raised in the 1950s and 1960s. I grew up in the 1960s and there were no morals and you would do whatever you wanted and authority was to be done away with. That's how it was.

• Well, we probably grew up on different sides of the 1960s then.

• But, overall culturally, if you wanted to do whatever you wanted then that was just fine just as long as you didn't hurt anybody else. The irony of it is that the same people who were doing that [in the 1960s] with no morals—or amoral, if you want to put it that way—are the same people who are primarily involved in these scandals. They are the people who are 45-55 years old, that you read about in the paper. It's a little bit different when you have the 25- to 30-year-olds in Silicon Valley, but certainly the things you hear about most often come from the people who were flower children. Maybe they think they can still do whatever they want.

• For me, it doesn't have to do with morals, but more with the fact that we've had a number of successive generations where it's difficult to point to a rallying point for us as a nation or us as a people, where personal interests get set aside in exchange for a common good. Unfortunately most of the examples you can point to are wars. In some of the reading I have done, there was a significant moral fiber that came as a byproduct from people having gone through World War I and World War II. Because individual interests and perspectives were set aside. It was almost an Eastern culture where it's the common good that drives actions at the expense of individual liberties—as opposed to individual liberty that comes before the common good.

• Countrywide, I think you're right. But up in Roseau you see what happened there [as a result of the floods of June 2002] or in the floods of the late 1990s, or with the forest fires in Arizona, or 9/11, there's an awful lot of good people who are concerned about their neighbors.

• There's a regional effect there too. I think that it's more predominant in the Midwest than it is on the coasts. I have a number of relatives who live on both coasts who like to come back here in the summer. They say we take our lifestyle for granted. I've lived in the same neighborhood for about seven years and they've lived in the same neighborhood for 15 to 20 years and they still don't know the people who live across the street. It just doesn't seem like you do that in California or on the East Coast. I know all of my neighbors, we eat dinner on each other's front porches. It's a Midwestern thing.

• For me though, it is more about awareness. Using 9/11 as an example, for six months we were all New Yorkers because all of that was placed right in front of us and we were so aware of it. How many didn't shed tears over that? How many people are aware of the flooding that is going on in Roseau? To what degree? And if you ramp up that awareness you're going to be impacted by it. But as that awareness is minimized, very few people are effected by that or are aware of it, so there is not the kind of broadly visible response. We don't have a whole lot of understanding about the individual pieces. We see isolated incidents and that effects the way we feel. It goes back to a degree about how well we know those around us and how well we interact.

• Sometimes I wonder if it isn't just a byproduct of the fact that we compartmentalize our lives much more than we used to. There is a part that's your work side and a part that's your home side and your family side, and then there's your community side, and then there might be your faith side. But it's not necessarily seen as a collective. When I'm with my neighbor I might act as a very ethical person, but when I go to work and push comes to shove, that's a different situation because it's work. As compared to it's who we are at our very moral fiber, because I think in some ways we are forced to be different people at different times and so you lay a different set of standards on them.

• Work has become aggressively separate from everyday life. It's the place that you go, and where you do the activity that brings you the money, and you participate in the rest of that value structure outside of the work setting. It is becoming progressively more and more distinct. And my faith and work and community all become very, very separate. Of all of them, I think that faith is the hardest to integrate.

• And cities have gotten bigger. It used to be that you owned a small company in a small city, and I owned the grocery store and I live next to him and he comes in and buys stuff from me and we all work together. Compared to now, if I live in downtown Minneapolis and work in Maple Grove and deal with people in New York City, you have no commonality. It didn't used to be like that. I couldn't be a different person in my grocery store than I could be as a neighbor. You can't make those distinctions because the farther apart you get physically, you can be different people in different parts of your life.

• At work to see a situation that is not morally ethical you may or may not say something about it because you want to keep your job. If you don't like that situation, your hands might be tied.

• I feel that when I look back at my parents, and I do feel that their generation had more focus in common compared to individualistic. But a lot of it was that they grew up in a small town and it was all German Catholic. But some of it was fear-based. I think that one of the positive things as a society is that we are saying that whatever my Christian values are, I don't want to inflict those on you, and yes it is OK for individuals to do their own thing, pursue their own path, so that's the positive side. Even given that we need to have some sort of overriding set of humanistic values we can all agree on regardless of our religion, but I don't think we know what those are and I don't know who's responsible for teaching them. I don't think that it's just about parents or churches. I think it's about who you are and what you reinforce through other means.

• I think that everybody knows what those values are. I do. I think that there's a sense that people know there are ethical standards and that there are morals and that there's a certain minimal level of acceptable behavior.

• But some people have that more than others. And some people don't have the tools to know when to say no and when not to [do something].

• I don't disagree with that. I don't necessarily think that people always practice, or participate, or that they don't sometimes choose to look the other way, but I think everybody has morals.

• I think people feel leeway to make personal choices, and I feel perfectly comfortable making those choices. It happens on the lowest scale—people park in handicapped spots all of the time and they know they shouldn't do that. Why? Because I'm only going to be in here for 5 minutes!

• But it's not because I don't know.

• Yeah. I know that's a minor, silly example, but it's people justifying that it's different because it's me.

• If we can go up higher than the handicapped parking spot,

when I think of my parents and I think of my grandparents, everyone believed the same sort of things, not necessarily religious, but more that they had the same values wherever you went. We've got such a pluralistic society now. And everyone has said, "Well, let John believe what he wants, everything is fine, you don't impose your own view on him and he doesn't his view on me." How much of that has to do with it? If John and I are going to do something. John says, "Well, he's my boss and this is what we're going to do. And I say, "Well, this is what I believe, but who am I to impose my values onto John?"

• So you're willing to give up on your values?

• We accept everybody for whatever they believe it seems like. I think I have strong values about myself. You know, it's like what you were talking about, but John can believe what he wants, he can do what he wants and as long as he doesn't hit my nose, he can do whatever he wants.

• That's interesting because it presumes that it's an unchallenged acceptance. You and I never get to have a dialogue about the difference between our two perspectives; we just don't challenge each other. There's never an effort that goes to getting to know the middle ground. There's never an effort that goes to getting to know the individual because that perspective will change.

• Who am I to tell them what is right or wrong?

• It's almost as if we don't ask a question in fear of offending somebody just by posing the question.

• It's interesting because you're being both very oversensitive and completely insensitive.

• When you are talking about finding words to describe things, I think that's one of things that we have not found, the words to talk about differences. We say it's not okay to talk about differences, but we haven't talked about how you could say, 'I'm sorry for being such and idiot, but let me ask you why you don't eat meat", or whatever the reason or the particular thing is. We haven't given people the permission or given them the right words to talk about it.

• There's a thing that all psychology classes talk about and that is that the opposite of love and hate isn't hate and love but indifference. You hit on a theory of either overly sensitive or insensitive, but there is this area in the middle where you're nothing.

• I think that there could be something there but we tend to focus on the extremes.

• Yeah, exactly.

• But in some ways it's not tolerance, it's indifference.

Let's talk about hiring practices for a little bit. If someone came in for an interview and they went out of their way to mention their faith, what's your reaction?

• I'd say uncomfortable.

• I'd agree.

• I am not uncomfortable because it's wrong, [but] because it's just one of those topics on the black list for political correctness.

• We aren't supposed to look at religion as a hiring criteria. It's a law. So we train our managers to keep it job-related, so I would expect a manager to step around that or shy away from that.

What if a person brings it up?

• I wouldn't want to go there.

• What do you say: "I don't want to hear you"?

• I would say, "That's interesting," and move on.

• I think that you can have discussions about your values without ever incorporating what church you attend.

• You can talk about examples of behavior.

• For me, it wouldn't be that tough. If it comes up, then I end up saying, "Well, that's kind of neat," and try to scoot around it. If it comes up again and again, then I end up saying, "You're on a topic I can't cover with you because it's against the law." If it doesn't stop at that point, then you're not getting hired because you're not following directions.

• Where I used to work, the board was engaging itself in hiring a new executive director. And they had a public conversation that I just blanched at because one of the resumés that they were considering, the guy went to a Bible college. And they were unsure about him as a candidate because he went to a Bible college. I was just alarmed by that. The fact that they had this whole discussion clearly seeing that word made them uncomfortable in one way or another.

What if an employee of your company brought up their faith as it related to their ethics and values in the workplace—how do you integrate that conversation into the workplace then?

• I think that it is a cultural opportunity because it is a time to understand what it is that you are not able to do and then what are the other options?

• To me, the critical part would be to separate how they express their faith versus that part which is about a truly ethical decision. I would separate those two things apart so you could get to the true issue.

• I think that's the same thing whether you're talking about a specific condition or some family constraints or whatever.

Do you think that it's more difficult for someone who is strongly committed to his or her religion to compete in today's business world?

• I think it depends on who you are as an individual.

• I don't think so.

• I don't know it there's a clean answer to that. I can look at two examples that fit your scenario that have answers at completely opposite ends.

• I hope that it doesn't. I think that it's the same as a number of other lifestyle choices. There are a number of other lifestyles that could fit just as easily into that scenario and you would hope that any of them wouldn't affect. I don't think so.

Chapter 6

Focus Group D

In our earlier sessions, somebody said that there is a certain incompatibility in talking about the relationship between the church, or spirituality and the workplace or between business and organized religion. What do you think of that? Is your spiritual life incompatible with what you do for a living?

• It depends on what you're doing for a living.

• I don't see it as incompatible, but I think there is a fine distinction that needs to be made in order for you to be a professional in the workplace. I don't think it's OK for me to be walking around and telling all of my colleagues and all of my clients my personal views because that could be a disservice to my employer. That's not what I expect, but at the same time I am a person with spiritual beliefs and I can't just set them aside when I walk in at work.

Is there a philosophical incompatibility between a spiritual person and a successful business person in terms of the tensions that you get from succeeding in business versus having a successful spiritual life?

• I don't think so.

• I don't think so.

• I've never felt like I was called on to be immoral or anything at work.

• I would agree. Or that I was asked to do something that went against my beliefs.

• No, never.

• Not in my professional life either.

• In fact it seems like to me that I am called on to bring out the best that's in me.

Is that the nature of this particular place to work or is it true elsewhere as well?

• Apparently it's true elsewhere. I think that there are a variety of types of businesses in my life and my spirituality helps me say how I'm going to do work because it helps keep me honest and it helps keep me doing what I do to do the best I can.

Have you ever witnessed the behavior of someone else in business that was not compatible with the way you think things should be done? And if so, what does one do about that ethically?

• Well, I've seen it in lots of ways. I think it shows in the way managers treat employees, in the way sales people deal with their customers, either ethically or unethically. What matters is how you deal with it, and that depends on your position in the organization or the person you are disagreeing with or challenging. I would say at times that wasn't a battle that I wanted to fight and at times I have confronted it.

What guides that decision?

• I think for me, part of it is the behavior that I am exhibiting or the way that I'm behaving contrary to the stated values of the business, or is it consistent with the state of values of the business? If it's contrary then its incentive or justification, I think. Hey, this is what we say we're about, what I just witnessed it doesn't seem like it agrees with what we say we're about.

But what guides it? Is there a spiritual aspect to it, or is it just plain old common-sense ethics?

• Just plain old common-sense ethics. In working in business, I don't know that I've thought spiritually about anything that I've done at work.

• There's an overlap between my spirituality and common-sense ethics. I don't have to go to my colleague and say, "I think that Jesus would do this in this situation" because you say, "Here's the deal," and that just makes sense.

What do you do with a circumstance or a setting when someone brings religion into the conversation at work? You can go outside your experience here.

• Well, my response would probably be, "That's great!" But these are either the guidelines, or this is the way I am choosing to handle it. It doesn't matter if they say Jesus or Buddha, or any other religion.

• I don't think that I have been called on to do anything that's dishonest in my work that I can think of—ever. So, I have never had to think about my spirituality. I am expected to do an honest job and always have been. I think it just goes back to what was said earlier about how it's so ingrained in you that you don't seem to separate it. I think that decisions that you make during the day are tied to your spirituality, but you're just not used to thinking about it that way.

• Back to your specific question though, how would I deal with that if somebody invoked the name of a spiritual authority of some kind. First of all, I would question it. If you do that, you're interpreting what you think that person or that being would want you to do in that particular situation. So, I kind of reject that overall approach. It would seem as though there's a little bit of an agenda there. First of all, you don't know what Jesus would do in this particular situation; we can infer, but that is best we can do. What's objectively right? This isn't a Christian issue, it's not a Buddhist issue—what is right for us as an organization, what's right for us as people, what's right for our customer, or whatever the situation may be. If somebody tried to inject or interject religion to that extent, I think I would be resistant. Pretty uniformly, that's just a guess.

• My tendency would be to raise an eyebrow or internally sigh or raise an eyebrow for that person and then continue on, but I wouldn't get engaged in the conversation. I think I'd avoid any kind of challenge or discussion. I'd just try to get out of the conversation.

• There are perfectly nice ethical people who don't really have any religious beliefs, and who are probably agnostic or something like that, but if you came up to them and said, "This is what Jesus would do," it seems seem as though you would kind of be confronting them, like you were trying to start an argument or something.

• But you know, I think a lot of people may see that as their obligation, like they're fundamental about it, like that's kind of the deal, here's the battlefield and your battlefield is the workplace and your job is to fight the battle for Mohammed or Christ.

• You know, I don't know if this is strange, I think I have heard others saying that they have never been put in the position of having to dispute that type of comment before, but I'll use my mother as an example. My mother is a very, very strict Lutheran parishioner. And she takes the word seriously and every day passes on the word of God, in every possible form she can, especially when she is confronted with an unethical situation or where she feels as though she is being confronted with one. So, she could be that person, especially if she is that firm on the act that is being done. She would say, "Well, Jesus told me to do that", and she'd be very serious about it and she will fight you if you were to dispute that. But, her motivation is not the business end of it, it's to talk about it and to bring it up and to be able to talk about religion in the workplace. That would be her motivation. I've never been confronted with that at work—only when I'm at home.

• One of our coworkers was diagnosed with cancer and we actually had a service for healing at the workplace. It was one evening, we got dinner together as a large group, and there was a Catholic priest that this guy had a relationship with in the past, and he flew up from New Mexico to do this. And we had a service for healing in our large conference room.

Did anyone think it was inappropriate for a business setting?

• That particular business, no. But it was a more spiritual kind of place to begin with. It was more consistent with the culture of the organization and the stated values and some other kinds of things.

• How many times have we seen e-mail passed around here saying, "Please pray for so and so." Being the office manager, I would probably be one of the first people to hear if someone had a issue with that. And no one has raised it here.

One of the questions we asked in the poll was as a business executive, you are a facing a serious business situation and have to make a critical decision that effects your business. Who would you talk to? I want to pose that question to you. There are five options, would you: A) talk to a colleague, B) talk to your spouse, C) talk it over with a spiritual or religious leader, D) pray to God for help or inspiration, E) or go off by yourself to meditate?

Eighty eight percent said they would talk it over with a colleague; the second-greatest response was that they would pray to God for help. Does that surprise anyone?

• Yes.

• Well, considering their options, I don't know that I am surprised. If it was talk to your colleague, talk to your investment banker, or talk to other business-oriented people, I'd be surprised if praying would get such a high response. But I guess I think what does your pastor know about business? It makes more sense to take it home and reflect, or read a quick prayer than to go sit down with your well-schooled priest who doesn't know anything about accounting.

• Just a side comment to what you just said there. It's surprising how many people will talk to their pastor about business deals and things that they're contemplating and going through, and it's not because they think [the pastor] understands the business. It's more a person's spiritual support in what they are doing and support in what they are contemplating about moral kinds of decisions and that kind of stuff.

• If they are thinking about doing the right thing.

• Sometimes it helps to talk to someone totally away from it so that they're not biased by anything.

What about when we look at Enron or the rest of the current culprits? One of the folks we interviewed in the first focus group knew some of the main players in Enron, and he said he knew them to be serious, Christian people who didn't think they were doing anything wrong. What's your sense of that in terms of your own experience or what your instinct tells you? Is it a lack of a moral business compass in the businessplace or is it simply a lack or morality in the businessplace?

• Sometimes people are so wrapped up in the pursuit of being successful and making the dollar that they sometimes overlook the moral aspect or make it so that they can be able to justify it and say it's OK.

How easy is it for us to delude ourselves into doing the best thing, just because it's the easiest thing?

• I think it's very easy for us to delude ourselves, but not necessarily for that reason. When I look at a case like Enron, I wonder if the question of is this right or wrong even ever occurred to them. It was: How can we make more money? And I think it was about how can the individuals make more money? This wasn't about how it had an impact on the corporate performance, but I think it was really motivated by greed. I wonder if that question even came up, and secondly, I think people get persuaded to do things that they wouldn't normally do—not necessarily in pursuit of profit, but an unwillingness to challenge leadership. We could name lots of historical events where large groups of people were persuaded to do things that were illegal, immoral, or whatever, because they were afraid to challenge those in power. Is there a spiritual component there? I think so. Where do you put your trust, where do you put your allegiance—as an individual, or is it in God, or some sort of religious figure?

• Well, the job description for a lot of CEOs is that they have to enhance shareholder value. Which means to make the bottom line look good.

We asked the business executives in the poll to describe something that comes closest to their beliefs. We didn't offer a definition of any of these, but we asked if they were religious, spiritual, spiritual but not religious, or neither. What would you anticipate that breakdown would be?

• At the executive level? I would guess spiritual but not religious.

• I would say that religious was the first one.

It was 53 percent religious and 36 percent spiritual but not religious.

• You know, there's one thing that I noticed when I left home for college and then in my first real job out of college. I was astonished by the number of people who were very out there about their religious beliefs. The students I went to school with who you would never have guessed. They were very open, in the fact that they were not trying to hide the fact that they were Christian (most were Catholic). But I was just very surprised. I would see people handle their daily activities or their daily jobs and sometimes what I see contradicts them saying, "I am a believer in the Lord and I am Christian and I go to church every Sunday or two or three times a week." That just surprises me for whatever reason because they don't conduct themselves that way. I think that includes everything from swearing to not just being ethical and moral.

Let's talk about that a little more. What is the appropriateness of talking about religion in the workplace?

• Years ago when I first started working, you pretty much knew what everybody's religion was. As time goes by, people don't talk about their religion anymore because it's probably not politically correct. Back in the 1960s, I knew what everybody's religion was in the whole place and you just don't know that anymore.

• I think that things were a little better when people would talk about their religion.

If somebody did it here would it be considered inappropriate?

• People do it here.

• I don't hear too much about it, but once in a while I guess I do. But back in the 1960s, they would come to work on Monday and sit there and go over everything that was said at the mass. Everybody in my department was Catholic except me. They would sit and talk about what was said at church the day before.

What if you were looking at a prospective employee who during an interview, without any prompting, volunteered that he

or she was a Christian? Is that a positive or a negative or doesn't it matter?

• On the record, it matters because there are some legal issues there. I think that if they were equal in every other respect, a person who said they were Christian might subconsciously be more likely to get a little bit of an upper hand in our office. Just because we tend to be more attracted to people who are more similar to us, the more we are similar to people, the more likely we are to have affiliation to them. It's not like we would say think, "Oh, he's a Christian, we've got to hire this guy." But I think that there are some unwanted processes that make that happen sometimes. People are attracted to other people like them.

• I could go either way on that depending on what the context was. Was it a natural extension of a conversation, or was it thrown out there as an interview gimmick? Was it real, was it genuine? So if I felt like it was contrived, I could see tipping the scale in favor of the other person, frankly.

I recently heard about a company that employs two people whose only job is praying for the company. What's your sense of that?

• I am very surprised by that. I guess I've never even heard of that before.

• There would probably be a few less Enrons around.

• I have met a couple guys at a conference who worked for a company that was founded by a born-again Christian and they were very overt—I mean it was on the Web site: This is who we are, this is our culture. They had a full-time chaplain on staff. It was an auto parts manufacturing company. Surprise was my first reaction and then part of it is you start to go, you know, that is a little much for me. And then I fight that notion too. I get into this battle with myself where I go: Is this weird? Is this bad? Is this OK? Is this great? I can't decide. I don't see anything wrong with it, but in this country you have to think about the kind of dynamics it creates inside the workplace: Is it fair and equitable? I think it makes it really unfair and difficult for people.

• When it's carried to that extreme, I think that a businessplace is a place of business. When you carry it to that extreme, I think that it would be distracting.

• If this company were to say, "We're going to hire this person to pray for our company," it certainly wouldn't make me behave any differently, or think of the company any differently, or of the CEO any differently.

• I would. I would think they're a bunch of quacks and that's the last thing I need from you right now. I mean I don't need somebody doing the rain dance over here.

• That's what would impact me: The other people in this office who would react to it—then I would have to react to it.

• Well, it's an interesting notion talking about praying for the company. I could see why companies would want to have chaplains on staff—the employees bring their issues to work, and so just as you've got an employee assistance program to help people deal with chemical dependency issues or other life stresses, you could have a spiritual leader who helped them with those issues.

What if, just as we were about to start this focus group I had said, "Let's everybody join hands for a prayer?" Would you have done it?

• I would be uncomfortable with that.

• I would do it. I agreed to be a person in this meeting, whatever that all meant.

• I would feel uncomfortable because in the e-mail I was told that I could be atheist and just show up.

What if a respected client of your company did it?

• I would stand up and pray.

• That doesn't say anything about me. I mean doing that, whether it's Buddhist, Hindu, it doesn't matter to me. I appreciate the fact that they are religious, to do that, and they are not asking me to convert, they are not asking me to do anything other that to just stand up and pray, so why not?

Let's talk about the church a little bit. I have been surprised by the feeling on behalf of the business community that there isn't much out there for them in terms of resources within the church. You have senior groups, parent groups, singles groups. The church caters to virtually every aspect of society except the business community. What are your feelings on that?

• I think that there is a presence there, but I've got a biased opinion. Because you know we've got men's groups that would be businessmen coming together to do Bible study breakfasts and social gatherings and a variety kinds of things.

• I think those opportunities are there, it's just up to you to bring up a specific topic that you want to discuss.

• But it is something where you have to say, "I want to talk business now," as opposed to going to the group that is specifically for women with children under the age of three. I don't know that there are groups that specifically address those issues.

• There are no workshops or Bible studies about running an ethical business sponsored by the church. I think I'd agree with that. It's an interesting notion because the vast majority of people in the church congregation are—percentage-wise—probably going to be working in companies.

• To me, that's where who you are and what your belief is comes in. There isn't a separation between who you are as a person and how you conduct your business. That whole being of who we are as a moral, ethical person—our spirituality dictates how we do our business, and it is pretty hard to separate the two.

• I am not sure where I would go. I know there's a men's group at church, and I imagine they talk about this every now and then, but not necessarily just about business.

Can you imagine a situation at work where you would counsel an employee about a personal problem in which spirituality would become part of the issue? Where is that line? Are there H.R. rules that prohibit it?

• Personally, I wouldn't force it; in fact, I would ask it before talking about it. Something to the effect of, "I don't know if you are a religious person." To which I would expect them to say no or give some sign of whether I can keep going or should stop right there. I would feel comfortable doing that, but then it depends on who we are talking to and the situation.

• Our company does not have any rules prohibiting it. There

are speaking guidelines, but they're not rules.

• I don't know if there are any rules; they are all guidelines and also those would state that you should use your best judgment.

• If I was a manager and a person came to me who was really struggling with a decision to leave the company or maybe something internally related, I can certainly see a conversation where I would ask the question, "What do you believe?" If this were in a different setting, I would ask them, "How does this business decision impact who you are and what you believe in?" Or: "What do your beliefs tell you ought to believe in?" So I could see how it would happen, I don't think that I would take the position of, "If you're a Christian, you ought to do this."

• I think that's where the line comes down. As long as it's something that starts neutral or there is some point in the past where you can talk about the church and not worry about it. But there are a lot of people I just wouldn't do that to, because it's presumption on my part about their spirituality. And then if I walk in and sit down and say, "Why don't you pray with me for a while?", and I don't even know what this person's spirituality is, I've crossed the line at that point. You have to have some level of awareness to get there first.

One last question. What would it do to a corporate culture if an employee or employees have Bibles on their desks? What do you think about that person?

• I had this job, and it might be the fact that this young lady had some personal problems that may have had something to do with it, I don't know. Anyway, she got real religious and went to one of these fundamental-type churches and on her break, she would go into the break room and sit there and read her Bible. I guess she found out that some of the other employees were laughing at her and stuff and I just told her, "Audrey, it's your break, it's your Bible and it's your life and if you want to read your Bible, then go ahead". But, that didn't stop the other employees.

• For me, it goes back to the personal business area. I don't care if they have their gym bag in their office or their Bible. As long as they are not starting every conversation with a client with some reference to that. You know, every time you walk into their office they've got to preach the affirmative. There are a lot of things that show you are an individual, so as soon as you start pushing it, then it becomes less of a personal and more of a professional matter.

Chapter 7

Focus Group E

We asked the business executives we polled what values or characteristics were missing in today's society—both in business and in general. What would you say?

• Honesty.

• A sense of humor.

• A set of accounting methods.

• Selfishness is an issue.

• I have pretty much worked and lived all over the world and I'd say the erosion of commitment that I saw compared to when I was a child, I don't see it now. Particularly with younger people. It's so much me-me-me and now that it's just kind of creeping around in society today. Worse than that, people don't seem to be apologetic for it at all. They just kind of expect it. I guess it's our fault. We raised these younger folks, and I don't know what to do about it. I don't like it, we see it in our companies, we see it displayed every day. It's like the opposite of what Kennedy said, "What can we do for me today?" Everything else is not worthy.

• I think that the number-one problem is the widening schedule between the have and the have-nots. It's getting greater and greater, and it's coming to light with what is going on with industry, but there is a greater, wider gap causing huge turmoil in the United States right now. So much mistrust of big businesses, obviously politics, I mean sports. Where [are the] people we look up to anymore? I've got an 18-year-old son; what good examples can he look at? In sports, all you do is talk about drugs. Music talks that way all of the time. In business, all they are is "me." They don't care—they don't give a damn about the people, their employees, they care about themselves. Politics? Well, we know what's happening there.

• At my former company we had a very youthful group. The average age was right around 30, and I was shocked at the comments made, at least by a lot of them, that they sincerely believed there was absolutely nothing they can do about it. They cannot change the things that are bad. When I grew up, we believed we could change whatever we applied our effort to. A lot of our younger people didn't vote. They said, "It's out of our control, so we are going to quit trying—we're just going to enjoy this—and away we go." In society today, more people have [that attitude] more than ever before.

• People today are not accountable for their actions. It's always somebody else's fault.

• On the other hand, even our generation can do better. Our pastor gave us a scolding on Sunday about what each member of the church does with their talents . He's a pretty fiery guy. He said, "You lawyers out there, how many pro-bono cases do you take for people who need something in this church a year? I'm listening for the number." I told my wife, "Boy is he giving it to the lawyers." But he kept on going. He got around to the businessmen eventually too and I said, "Man, this is not fair now." But, he's a good point.

I am going to read a couple of items out loud and I'd like you to tell me if this is something you would or would not do. If you were facing a difficult, ethical business decision would you talk the situation over with your spouse or significant other?

- Always.

- I'd have to know if it is a confidential issue because I think that as executives there are a number of things that are brought to us in confidence and I would have to respect that.

- I'd say almost never. I am an old-school guy and I almost never bring my work home. A long time ago, I made a very early decision that [this is] my work and [this is my] family. It's bad enough that I spend too much time in this business. I close the door when I drive in the driveway and everything stays at work.

- I agree with you. If the decision's obvious, if you don't have to talk to anybody, then don't talk to anybody about it.

- I discuss work with my wife because she is a superior people person. She deals with people every day, all day and she has for 30 years. She has an insight to people that I can't even touch. Generally, the issues that come up are people problems.

- I have networked with people when I was running a company—peers and contemporaries. Most of the people that I share with I've done so because I relied on their judgment. A lot have them had been through similar experiences. I just kept my wife out of the business side of it. When I walked through the door, there were other things to talk about.

- I remember the first time that I moved from the corporate

headquarters to Chicago and people didn't like me much because we were from the guy that just bought the company. I felt terrible and alone and would be all by myself. Before I used to get up out of my chair and go down the hall and talk over some things with my colleagues. It's nice to have a good place that you can go or discuss those ideas or issues.

Is there ever a circumstance when you could take something like that to your religious leader? Would you ever turn to the church for answer or guidance in business?

• I never would for guidance.

• I never mix the two together. You can't bring the church issues in to the business because people have different denominations and different faiths, especially with diversity going on.

• I guess I'd say I'd turn to it but in a different way. There's a group of guys that I meet with—we don't exactly have a church relationship, but we definitely have a spiritual relationship—but that's not necessarily the same thing.

• I tend not to go to the church for my business challenges, but I know enough resources or areas that if I had a legal question, I know some particular attorneys that could help or I know accounting and financial people that I would go to. I don't know of a certain stance in ethics or circumstance where the church would be that resource.

• If it's a black and white thing that you're talking about, legal or financial, or that sort of thing, I wouldn't go there either. The thing that I find myself talking to a priest about are when I can't come down on something emotionally. That's the one thing that I like to talk to the priest about.

• I spent many years working for a company here in town. The CEO said something to us when I was a pretty young guy that really stuck with me. We were arguing one day about company policies and we got all emotionally wound up over a couple of things and in the end, somebody asked what he expected of us. He said, "I'll tell you what I expect of you. I am going to hold you accountable for your judgment. Don't ever come in here and hide behind a policy if that policy was deficient in its creation. So, in the end, I expect you guys to be experienced enough and wise enough to use good judgment." And that always stuck with me. Another situation that I'd turn to the clergy for help with is in the case of a circumstance we had here a while back. We had some Muslim folks beginning to work here and we had all kinds of problems because their religious behavior didn't fit with our company policy. At times like that, I would reach out to some clergy and ask for some educational help. I have been a member at a church here in Plymouth for many years and our pastor was an aggressive resource assigner. If you got a call from him, you knew there was a task that had to be done. He'd come across people who needed help for some reason—either with a struggling business or personal financial issues. And he put together these little teams and then he would call you up and would advise you to be put on the team. You didn't dare say no. And this guy was really a dynamo; he knew everything that everybody had for talents and he could pluck them out in little clusters. I could name eight or 10 people right now who worked long and hard on problems in our community because of him.

Do you feel as though you could turn to the church? That you would find a resource there that would know enough about business to be able to give you counsel in a that sense?

• I'd say yes.

• No, I don't think so. There are more pastors of churches that I've belonged to in the past who wouldn't have a clue how to help. But I think that a really active pastor who really understands his parishioners and their talents would be, should be able to know what resources are available to them and if they don't—shame on them. I'll share a very interesting story with you. When a friend of mine started his first business in Russia, he was a friend of the former pastor of Hennepin. One day he calls him up and asked if the pastor had anybody in the church who knew something about farming. The pastor said he did and that he was the CEO of Land O'Lakes." So he phoned him up, and the CEO said he was getting ready to retire. But the pastor pushed and the CEO made a trip over there. That was 10 years ago and he now is in charge of the largest farming operation in Russia. And he did it under the co-op organization approach that Land O'Lakes used. You know, it was all because the pastor knew what talents he had in his community and knew what to ask. I think that is a minimum requirement of a staff of a parish.

• That's a little different take on that. My take on it was would you go to him with problems and what you are describing or what I hear you describing is a networking sort of guy who is able to make connections and drag out resources. It's interesting, because when I think of a minister, I wouldn't expect him to understand the manufacturing business for example, or the selling business, or that type of thing. I would probably expect him to understand personal problems, but that would be as much as I would expect a pastor to understand.

What about the issue of accountability within a corporation or a business? Who's responsibility is it to be the ethical watchdog? Is it a personal responsibility or a collective one?

• The people you employ and the leadership you get has to be pretty consistent.

• You lead by example.

So then what happens when the upper-level executives of a company—I'm thinking of the recent headlines—aren't acting ethically?

• Go get a job someplace else.

• Don't work there. As long as you work there, you're part of the problem.

• People hang on to jobs for some very good reasons and sometimes it's not right to take off. I agree—if you're going to complain about it, then you are rooting yourself to be part of the problem.

• If anybody sees anything unethical it should be reported to somebody.

• The real issue is we tend to choose examples that are on the outer extreme edges. I think that it is far more important for people within a company who see things that are inappropriate who choose to say nothing first of all, and stay anonymous. But being judgmental and critical is never-ending. That to me is every bit as incorrect and that person is every bit as guilty as the perpetrator on top of the company. Another alternative would be working for change within the company—patiently working at and setting the different examples. Companies change because of their people. The idea that "those guys up on top are the guys who need to make a change and I'm going to sit on my duff until they do" is just repulsive to me.

• I agree with you. The dilemma I see is just dealing with nebulous terms that we haven't defined. "Moral" and "ethical" are different in every company. So if I come to work for your company, what's moral and what's ethical and what's the tolerance level for that? To put it very simply, we do not allow employee theft in our company. We will not tolerate an employee taking home the welding torches and six 2 by 4s to build a shed. That is absolutely forbidden. Companies define those kinds of limits, those kinds of disciplines and what becomes moral and ethical in the company. It's really hard because most companies don't define it well.

• So it becomes: What's the ethic for that business or that company? Some are very rigid—every new employee and every employee knows what they are when they come in and they are structured and you know if you lie, you've crossed an ethical line. But most of the companies I've come in contact with are not well-defined. So it's left to all of the various judgments of employees.

• I hear what you're saying and it's like our laws. I think this has a lot to do with companies and using basic common sense. How would you like to be treated, how would you like to treat other people, and what would you like with your company? What would do if it was your company? Think of it that way.

Is there an incompatibility between being a spiritual person or a religious person and being successful in business?

• I don't think so.

• I am going to treat people how they want to be treated. There's got to be some moral ground. I would say that we need to be very honest with people so they always know what they are getting.

• My biggest customer in Oklahoma City and it's a really religious company and they hold 300 stores and they have two signs on the wall that say you can not take employees out to lunch or to dinner because they must be with their families. It's quite a company. You can't buy them any gifts. Everything is very up front. All of their stores are closed on Sundays throughout the country. It's a very big part of their company.

• There's a degree of understanding there. I think employees value business leadership that is principal, ethical, and fair. I think if they were truthful, they would tell you they have less respect for business leaders who are irresponsible—cheating on their wives, blowing up their expense accounts, all that kind of stuff. I think also that people look to the management of companies to demonstrate their values in how they make decisions every day. They're frequently turned off by people who wear religion on their sleeve who are constantly advising everybody that they're a born-again Christian and then, in the afternoon take unfair advantage of a situation and rip somebody off. People are smarter than they get credit for. They see that. Practicing it however, reaching out to help people, setting examples, I don't think people see that negatively. I think they see it respectfully.

Chapter 8

Selected Crosstabs

The following pages contain the crosstabs—a breakdown of the poll results by demographic categories. An abbreviated version of each question is listed at the top of each page and the crosstabs are displayed in one, two or three columns. The numbers are the same in each column; they are simply rank-ordered on different categories to highlight which groups scored highest and lowest on these different categories. An asterisk indicates there are less than 30 people in that subgroup, therefore, the data for that subgroup is not as significant as data for subgroups with 30 or more people.

Question 6
Business Decisions: Talk it Over With a Colleague at Work?

1. Would: 82
2. Would Not: 15
3. No Opinion/Refused: 3

Would		**Would Not**		**No Opinion/Refused**	
Employ: 101-250	97-3-0	Raised: Luth	70-28-3	Raised: Pres	68-21-12
*Den: Ath/Agn	92-8-0	*Den: Luth	71-25-4	Den: Pres	78-13-9
18-34	90-9-1	Exec: 15-25 Yrs	75-23-2	Den: Bapt	70-20-9
Exec: 5-10 Yrs	89-9-2	Raised: Bapt	73-21-6	Employ: 11-25	80-13-7
Employ: 250+	89-10-1	Employ: 4-10	76-21-3	*Den: Non-Chr	73-20-7
Raised: Meth	88-12-0	Raised: Presb	68-21-12	*Raised: Non-Chr	75-19-6
Raised: Oth Chr	88-9-3	Den: Bapt	70-20-9	Exec: 25+ Yrs	74-20-6
Raised: No Relig	87-11-2	*Den: Non-Chr	73-20-7	35-44	81-13-6
Employ: 26-100	87-11-3	55-64	79-20-2	Raised: Bapt	73-21-6
Exec: <5 Yrs	86-11-3	Exec: 25+ Yrs	74-20-6	Post-Grad Deg	84-10-6
Men	86-12-2	Very Conserv	79-19-2	Northeast	81-14-6
65+	86-12-2	Women	76-19-5	Exec: 10-15 Yrs	79-15-6
Den: None	86-12-3	*Raised: Non-Chr	75-19-6	Women	76-19-5
Raised: Cath	85-12-2	Some Coll/Voc	80-19-1	College Grad	81-14-5
West	85-12-3	*Den: Meth	81-19-0	45-54	78-17-5
Den: Oth Chr	85-13-3	South	81-18-1	Midwest	81-14-5
Post-Grad Deg	84-10-6	Born-Again: Yes	78-18-4	Born-Agn: Yes	78-18-4
Den: Cath	83-14-2	45-54	78-17-5	Somewhat Cons	83-13-4
Somewhat Cons	83-13-4	Independents	82-16-2	Democrats	80-15-4
Rpblcns	83-14-4	HS or Less	82-16-2	Rpblcns	83-14-4

Question 7
Business Decisions: Talk it Over With Your Spouse?

1. Would: 65
2. Would Not: 30
3. No Opinion/Refused: 5

Would		Would Not		No Opinion/Refused	
Employ: 26-100	79-20-1	*Den: Non-Chr	47-53-0	*Den: Ath/Agn	52-36-12
*Den: Meth	78-22-0	Employ: 250+	48-49-3	65+	60-29-11
Den: Bapt	77-18-5	*Raised: Non-Chr	50-44-6	Employ: 101-250	55-35-10
Den: Oth Chr	77-20-3	Den: None	53-39-8	Post-Grad Deg	63-28-9
*Den: Luth	75-25-0	Democrats	55-38-8	Employ: 11-25	62-30-9
Exec: 10-15 Yrs	74-25-1	*Den: Ath/Ag	52-36-12	Neither Con/Lib	58-33-8
Exec: 15-25 Yrs	73-23-4	Employ: 101-250	55-35-10	Northeast	61-31-8
Raised: Luth	73-28-0	Den: Presb	63-34-3	Den: None	53-39-8
Raised: Oth Chr	72-25-3	Raised: Cath	59-34-7	Democrat	55-38-8
Born-Agn: Yes	72-23-5	Neither Cons/Lib	58-33-8	Raised: Catholic	59-34-7
Raised: Meth	71-23-6	Some Coll/Voc	64-33-3	Exec: <5 Yrs	60-33-7
Employ: 4-10	71-25-4	35-44	62-33-5	Den: Cath	61-32-7
Born-Agn: No	70-27-2	Exec: 25+ Yrs	61-33-6	Raised: No Relig	63-30-7
Midwest	70-26-5	Exec: <5 Yrs	60-33-7	College Grad	65-29-6
Very Cons	70-29-1	South	61-33-6	*Raised: Non-Chr	50-44-6
HS or Less	70-27-3	Den: Cath	61-32-7	South	61-33-6
Rpblcns	69-26-5	Exec: 5-10 Yrs	64-31-5	Exec: 25+ Yrs	61-33-6
West	69-29-2	55-64	66-31-3	Somewhat Cons	66-28-6
Independents	68-28-4	Liberal	65-31-4	Raised: Presb	65-29-6
45-54	68-27-5	Northeast	61-31-8	Raised: Meth	71-23-6

Question 8
Business Decisions: Talk With a Spiritual or Religious Leader?

1. Would: 33
2. Would Not: 63
3. No Opinion/Refused: 4

Would		Would Not		No Opinion/Refused	
Born-Agn: Yes	62-34-4	*Den: Ath/Agn	4-92-4	*Raised: Non-Chr	13-75-13
Very Cons	51-44-5	Den: None	16-81-3	Raised: Oth Chr	40-53-7
Den: Bapt	50-43-7	*Den: Non-Chr	13-80-7	Den: Bapt	50-43-7
Den: Oth Chr	49-45-6	Employ: 250+	23-76-1	Employ: 11-25	32-62-7
Den: Presb	47-47-6	*Raised: Non-Chr	13-75-13	*Den: Non-Chr	13-80-7
65+	45-52-3	Raised: No Rel	22-74-4	Employ: 101-250	23-71-6
Exec: 25+ Yrs	44-54-2	Liberal	24-74-3	Den: Presb	47-47-6
HS or Less	43-55-2	College Grad	21-73-5	Neither Con/Lib	27-67-6
*Den: Luth	43-57-0	Employ: 101-250	23-71-6	Raised: Presb	32-62-6
Raised: Bapt	41-59-0	Raised: Cath	28-70-2	Den: Oth Chr	49-45-6
Employ: 4-10	41-57-2	Exec: 5-10 Yrs	27-70-3	Northeast	30-65-6
Raised: Oth Chr	40-53-7	Born-Agn: No	28-70-2	College Grad	21-73-5
Raised: Luth	40-55-5	Den: Cath	30-69-1	45-54	36-59-5
Women	37-60-3	18-34	27-69-5	Very Cons	51-44-5
Some Coll/Voc	37-60-3	Emply: 26-100	30-67-3	Raised: Luth	40-55-5
*Den: Meth	37-63-0	35-44	31-67-2	18-34	27-69-5
Post-Grad Deg	36-60-3	Neither Con/Li	27-67-6	Raised: No Rel	22-74-4
45-54	36-59-5	Independents	30-66-4	Democrats	32-63-4
Rpblcns	36-61-3	Men	30-65-4	Exec: 10-15 Yrs	35-61-4
South	36-62-2	Smwt Cons	32-65-3	Exec: 15-25 Yrs	31-65-4

Question 9
Business Decisions: Pray to God for Help or Inspiration?

1. Would: 74
2. Would Not: 25
3. No Opinion/Refused: 1

Would		Would Not		No Opinion/Refused	
Born-Agn: Yes	96-4-0	*Den: Ath/Agn	32-68-0	*Den: Meth 89-7-4	
Den: Bapt	93-7-0	*Den: Non-Chr	33-67-0	Den: Presb	81-16-3
*Den: Meth	89-7-4	*Rsd: Non-Chr	38-63-0	Rsd: Presb	74-24-3
Den: Oth Chr	88-11-1	Rsd: No Rel	57-43-0	Rsd: Luth	70-28-3
Very Cons	85-14-1	Liberal	59-41-0	Rsd: Meth	83-15-2
Rsd: Bapt	84-16-0	Den: None	61-39-0	35-44	70-29-2
45-54	84-16-0	Coll Grad	67-32-1	65+	80-18-2
Rsd: Meth	83-15-2	West	68-32-0	Exec: 10-15 Yrs	76-22-1
*Den: Luth	82-18-0	18-34	69-31-0	Emply: 26-100	72-26-1
Rsd: Oth Chr	81-19-0	Neither Con/Lib	68-31-1	South	79-20-1
Den: Presb	81-16-3	55-64	69-31-0	Exec: 25+ Yrs	73-26-1
Smwt Cons	81-19-1	Dems	70-30-0	Neither Con/Lib	68-31-1
Women	81-19-0	Men	70-30-1	Northeast	69-30-1
Exec: 15-25 Yrs	80-19-1	Northeast	69-30-1	Post-Grad Deg	72-27-1
65+	80-18-2	Emply: 11-25	70-29-1	Exec: 15-25 Yrs	80-19-1
HS or Less	79-21-0	35-44	70-29-2	Very Cons	85-14-1
South	79-20-1	Exec: 5-10 Yrs	72-28-0	Den: Oth Chr	88-11-1
Some Coll/Voc	79-21-1	Exec: <5 Yrs	72-28-0	Emply: 11-25	70-29-1
Emply: 4-10	78-22-0	Emply: 250+	72-28-0	Repblcns	76-23-1
Midwest	77-23-0	Rsd: Luth	70-28-3	Men	70-30-1

Question 10
Business Decisions: Go Off by Yourself to Meditate?

1. Would: 61
2. Would Not: 39
3. No Opinion/Refused: 0

Would		Would Not		No Opinion/Refused	
Neither Con/Lib	70-29-1	*Rsd: Non-Chr	38-63-0	Emply: 101-250	52-45-3
Born-Agn: Yes	69-30-1	*Den: Meth	41-59-0	45-54	61-37-2
Den: Oth Chr	68-31-1	*Den: Non-Chr	47-53-0	Midwest	55-43-2
65+	68-32-0	Rsd: Meth	50-50-0	Neither Con/Lib	70-29-1
Rsd: Luth	68-33-0	Emply: 250+	51-49-0	Rsd: Oth Chr	67-32-1
Rsd: Oth Chr	67-32-1	Coll Grad	52-47-1	HS or Less	62-37-1
Very Cons	67-33-0	Rsd: Presb	53-47-0	Exec: 5-10 Yrs	62-37-1
Post-Grad Deg	66-34-0	Liberal	52-47-1	Emply: 11-25	62-38-1
Exec: 10-15 Yrs	65-35-0	Emply: 101-250	52-45-3	Independents	63-36-1
South	65-35-0	18-34	56-44-0	Den: None	59-40-1
Emply: 4-10	65-35-0	55-64	56-44-0	Den: Oth Chr	68-31-1
Den: Cath	64-36-0	Den: Presb	56-44-0	Women	55-44-1
Some Coll/Voc	64-36-0	Exec: 15-25 Yrs	56-44-0	Liberal	52-47-1
Dems	64-35-1	Women	55-44-1	Dems	64-35-1
Men	64-36-0	Midwest	55-43-2	Rsd: Cath	63-37-1
Independents	63-36-1	Northeast	57-43-0	Born-Agn: Yes	69-30-1
35-44	63-37-0	Smwt Cons	57-43-0	Exec: <5 Yrs	58-41-1
Rsd: Cath	63-37-1	*Den: Luth	57-43-0	Coll Grad	52-47-1
Exec: 5-10 Yrs	62-37-1	Repblcns	57-43-0	Aggregate	60-39-0
HS or Less	62-37-1	Born-Agn: No	58-42-0	Emply: 26-100	61-39-0

Question 11: (Split Sample)

Let's say you need to hire someone in your sales department. For the sake of the example, two men apply, Mr. A and Mr. B. If the following was all you knew about each one, which one would you probably hire? Mr. A is a top university grad with an A-avrg. He's single, well dressed, and articulate. He worked through college in fast-food. Mr. B is a state Coll Grad with a B average. He's newly married, looks nice, and is soft spoken. He worked summers in his dad's business.

1. Would Hire Mr. A: 34
2. Would Hire Mr. B: 49
3. No Opinion: 17

Hire Mr. A		Hire Mr. B		No Opinion	
*Rsd: Non-Chr	63-38-0	Rsd: Meth	20-64-16	*Den: Luth	17-50-33
*Den: Ath/Agn	57-36-7	Independents	16-63-20	Emply: 101-250	40-30-30
*Den: Non-Chr	57-43-0	Emply: 4-10	22-62-16	55-64	25-50-25
Post-Grad Deg	55-29-17	65+	34-62-3	Emply: 250+	39-37-24
18-34	48-43-10	HS or Less	18-62-20	Exec: 15-25 Yrs	26-51-23
Emply: 26-100	47-38-15	Exec: 10-15 Yrs	23-61-16	West	39-39-22
Emply: 11-25	47-43-10	Women	27-61-12	Rsd: Luth	33-44-22
Den: Presb	43-36-21	Some Coll/Voc	24-61-16	Northeast	31-46-22
Exec: <5 Yrs	43-41-16	Born-Agn: Yes	27-58-16	*Den: Meth	29-50-21
35-44	43-41-16	45-54	25-57-18	Den: Presb	43-36-21
Coll Grad	43-43-15	Den: Bapt	24-57-19	Independents	16-63-20
Repblcns	41-43-16	Midwest	34-54-12	Born-Agn: No	36-44-20
Den: Cath	40-47-13	Rsd: Bapt	32-54-14	HS or Less	18-62-20
Emply: 101-250	40-30-30	South	33-53-14	Men	39-41-20
Emply: 250+	39-37-24	Exec: 25+ Yrs	31-53-16	Den: Bapt	24-57-19
Men	39-41-20	Den: None	32-53-16	Rsd: Presb	38-44-19
West	39-39-22	Rsd: No Rel	30-52-17	Den: Oth Chr	30-52-19
Exec: 5-10 Yrs	38-49-13	Dems	35-52-13	Very Cons	31-51-18
Rsd: Presb	38-44-19	Den: Oth Chr	30-52-19	Neither Con/Lib	36-45-18
Born-Agn: No	36-44-20	Smwt Cons	36-52-13	Rsd: Cath	36-46-18

Question 12 (split sample)

Let's say you need to hire someone in your sales department. For the sake of the example, two men apply, Mr. A and Mr. B. If the following was all you knew about each one, which one would you probably hire? Mr. A is a top university graduate with an A- average. He's single, well dressed, and articulate. He worked through college in fast-food. He says he's not real religious. Mr. B is a state university grad with a B average. He's newly wed, looks nice, and is soft spoken. He worked summers for his dad and attends church.

1. Would Hire Mr. A: 27
2. Would Hire Mr. B: 51
3. No Opinion: 22

Hire Mr. A		Hire Mr. B		No Opinion	
*Den: Non-Chr	50-25-25	Born-Agn: Yes	8-77-14	*Rsd: Non-Chr	38-25-38
Northeast	44-41-15	Den: Bapt	13-74-13	*Den: Ath/Agn	36-27-36
Emply: 250+	44-32-24	Den: Presb	17-72-11	Independents	25-38-36
Liberal	43-37-20	Very Cons	18-70-12	Post-Grad Deg	33-35-33
Den: None	43-34-23	Rsd: Bapt	9-70-21	Neither Con/Lib	23-45-33
Rsd: Meth	41-52-7	*Den: Meth	15-69-15	Rsd: Oth Chr	25-44-31
Rsd: No Rel	39-39-22	Exec: 25+ Yrs	14-68-19	55-64	17-53-30
Exec: <5 Yrs	38-42-20	65+	17-67-17	Emply: 11-25	24-48-28
*Rsd: Non-Chr	38-25-38	Emply: 4-10	18-64-19	35-44	33-39-28
18-34	37-52-11	Rsd: Luth	27-64-9	Exec: 10-15 Yrs	29-44-27
*Den: Ath/Agn	36-27-36	Some Coll/Voc	24-59-17	South	20-55-25
Emply: 26-100	36-43-21	Repblcns	25-58-17	*Den: Non-Chr	50-25-25
Dems	33-50-17	Den: Oth Chr	24-58-18	HS or Less	23-52-25
35-44	33-39-28	Midwest	23-58-19	West	31-44-25
Post-Grad Deg	33-35-33	Rsd: Presb	22-56-22	*Den: Luth	31-44-25
*Den: Luth	31-44-25	Exec: 5-10 Yrs	22-55-22	Women	24-51-25
Born-Agn: No	31-47-22	South	20-55-25	Emply: 250+	44-32-24
Coll Grad	31-51-18	Den: Cath	23-53-23	Den: None	43-34-23
West	31-44-25	55-64	17-53-30	Den: Cath	23-53-23
45-54	30-48-22	Emply: 101-250	29-52-19	Exec: 15-25 Yrs	26-51-23

Question 13
Business Executives Obedience to Laws Governing Their Profession

1. Try To Obey The Laws: 70
2. Try To Find Way Around The Law: 25
3. No Opinion: 6

Obey Laws		Find Way Around		No Opinion	
Rsd: Presb	85-15-0	*Rsd: Non-Chr	50-38-13	*Den: Non-Chr	60-27-13
Den: Presb	84-16-0	Den: Oth Chr	61-33-7	*Rsd: Non-Chr	50-38-13
*Den: Meth	81-11-7	Dems	62-32-6	55-64	70-20-10
Rsd: Luth	78-18-5	HS or Less	61-31-8	Exec: 25+ Yrs	67-23-10
Emply: 250+	77-22-1	Rsd: No Rel	61-30-9	Post-Grad Deg	69-22-9
Exec: 15-25 Yrs	77-21-2	Born-Agn: Yes	64-30-6	Rsd: No Rel	61-30-9
Independents	77-17-6	Rsd: Bapt	66-30-4	Emply: 11-25	67-24-9
Rsd: Meth	77-21-2	Very Cons	63-29-8	Neither Con/Lib	65-26-8
Born-Agn: No	76-19-6	65+	63-29-8	Rsd: Oth Chr	68-24-8
Smwt Cons	76-20-4	Exec: 5-10 Yrs	66-29-5	Very Cons	63-29-8
Den: Cath	74-20-6	Emply: 26-100	66-29-5	*Den: Ath/Agn	68-24-8
Coll Grad	74-23-3	Liberal	68-28-4	HS or Less	61-31-8
Exec: 10-15 Yrs	74-19-7	35-44	71-28-1	65+	63-29-8
Repblcns	73-21-6	Exec: <5 Yrs	67-27-5	*Den: Meth	81-11-7
West	72-23-5	Midwest	67-27-6	Women	68-25-7
*Den: Luth	71-25-4	Den: None	67-27-6	Exec: 10-15 Yrs	74-19-7
35-44	71-28-1	*Den: Non-Chr	60-27-13	Den: Bapt	68-25-7
Emply: 101-250	71-26-3	Neither Con/Lib	65-26-8	Northeast	70-23-7
45-54	71-23-6	Emply: 101-250	71-26-3	Den: Oth Chr	61-33-7
Men	71-25-4	18-34	70-26-5	Rsd: Cath	69-25-6

Question 14
Frequency: Competitors Use Unethical Actions as Advantage? (part 1*)

1. Yes/Quite A Bit: 13
2. Yes/Occasionally: 27
3. Yes/Not Very Often: 18
4. Yes/No Opinion: 1
5. No: 40
6. No Opinion/Refused: 2

* Note: Crosstabs below are for categories 1, 2, and 3. Categories 4, 5, and 6 are on the next page.

Yes/Quite a Bit		Yes/Occasionally		Yes/Not Very Often	
*Den: Non-Chr	20-40-13	*Den: Non-Chr	20-40-13	*Den: Luth	4-25-25
Neither Con/Lib	19-27-21	*Rsd: Non-Chr	13-38-13	*Den: Ath/Agn	16-20-24
*Den: Meth	19-15-22	Rsd: Cath	11-36-20	Rsd: Meth	15-21-23
Exec: 15-25 Yrs	18-31-22	Emply: 101-250	13-35-16	Men	12-26-23
35-44	17-27-13	Exec: 10-15 Yrs	8-35-19	55-64	12-20-22
Emply: 11-25	17-29-18	Liberal	7-33-12	45-54	12-33-22
Independents	16-32-18	45-54	12-33-22	*Den: Meth	19-15-22
*Den: Ath/Agn	16-20-24	West	13-32-12	Exec: 25+ Yrs	16-22-22
Post-Grad Deg	16-30-16	Some Coll/Voc	13-32-21	Exec: 15-25 Yrs	18-31-22
Exec: 25+ Yrs	16-22-22	Independents	16-32-18	Neither Con/Lib	19-27-21
Den: Cath	16-28-21	Den: Oth Chr	13-32-13	Den: Cath	16-28-21
Rsd: Meth	15-21-23	Exec: 15-25 Yrs	18-31-22	South	12-26-21
Rsd: Presb	15-29-18	65+	11-31-12	Some Coll/Voc	13-32-21
Rsd: Oth Chr	14-24-20	18-34	9-30-15	Very Cons	12-27-20
Dems	14-25-11	Post-Grad Deg	16-30-16	Repblcns	11-29-20
Northeast	14-26-18	Rsd: Presb	15-29-18	Rsd: Cath	11-36-20
Born-Agn: No	14-25-19	Women	13-29-11	Rsd: Oth Chr	14-24-20
Some Coll/Voc	13-32-21	Emply: 26-100	9-29-16	Exec: 10-15 Yrs	8-35-19
Emply: 101-250	13-35-16	Emply: 11-25	17-29-18	Born-Agn: No	14-25-19
Smwt Cons	13-25-18	Den: None	9-29-15	Emply: 250+	11-24-19

Question 14
Frequency: Competitors Use Unethical Actions as Advantage? (part 2*)

1. Yes/Quite A Bit: 13
2. Yes/Occasionally: 27
3. Yes/Not Very Often: 18
4. Yes/No Opinion: 1
5. No: 40
6. No Opinion/Refused: 2

* Note: Crosstabs below are for categories 4, 5, and 6. Categories 1, 2, and 3 are on the previous page.

Yes/No Opinion		No		No Opinion/Refused	
Rsd: Luth	3-53-3	Rsd: Luth	3-53-3	Exec: 15-25 Yrs	1-24-4
Exec: 25+ Yrs	2-37-1	Den: Bapt	2-52-0	*Den: Ath/Agn	0-36-4
Den: Bapt	2-52-0	Dems	1-50-0	Coll Grad	0-44-4
Rsd: No Rel	2-48-2	Rsd: No Rel	2-48-2	Den: Oth Chr	2-38-4
Some Coll/Voc	2-32-0	Exec: 5-10 Yrs	0-48-0	Emply: 250+	0-42-4
Den: Oth Chr	2-38-4	Exec: <5 Yrs	1-47-2	*Den: Meth	0-41-4
55-64	2-42-2	Rsd: Bapt	0-47-1	Neither Con/Lib	1-27-4
65+	2-42-3	Den: None	0-47-0	West	1-38-3
Born-Agn: Yes	1-39-2	Liberal	1-47-0	Den: Presb	0-38-3
Neither Con/Lib	1-27-4	*Den: Luth	0-46-0	Rsd: Oth Chr	1-38-3
Northeast	1-40-1	HS or Less	1-46-2	65+	2-42-3
Den: Cath	1-33-1	Emply: 26-100	0-46-0	Repblcns	1-36-3
Exec: 15-25 Yrs	1-24-4	Women	0-45-2	Rsd: Presb	0-35-3
Men	1-36-2	18-34	0-44-1	35-44	0-40-3
Rsd: Oth Chr	1-38-3	Coll Grad	0-44-4	Rsd: Luth	3-53-3
Very Cons	1-37-2	55-64	2-42-2	Midwest	1-40-2
Emply: 4-10	1-40-2	Smwt Cons	1-42-2	Born-Agn: Yes	1-39-2
HS or Less	1-46-2	Emply: 250+	0-42-4	Rsd: No Rel	2-48-2
Emply: 11-25	1-34-1	65+	2-42-3	Smwt Cons	1-42-2
45-54	1-31-1	*Den: Meth	0-41-4	Exec: <5 Yrs	1-47-2

Question 15
Noticed Legal, Yet Unethical Actions/Mention to Coworker? (part 1*)

1. Yes/Usually Mention: 40
2. Yes/Usually Keep Quiet: 12
3. Yes/No Opinion: 3
4. No: 43
5. Refused: 2

* Note: Crosstabs below are for categories 1 and 2. Categories 3 and 4 are on the next page.

Yes/Usually Mention		Yes/Usually Keep Quiet	
Rsd: No Rel	54-7-2-37	*Den: Non-Chr	27-27-0-40
West	50-9-5-36	Emply: 101-250	42-26-6-26
Emply: 250+	49-19-4-28	*Rsd: Non-Chr	25-25-0-44
Rsd: Oth Chr	48-12-3-35	65+	43-22-2-34
Some Coll/Voc	46-11-1-40	Emply: 250+	49-19-4-28
Dems	46-14-2-35	Den: Presb	25-19-13-41
45-54	46-8-2-43	Rsd: Presb	32-18-9-38
Den: Oth Chr	44-12-1-41	Exec: <5 Yrs	36-17-3-39
Emply: 11-25	44-11-3-38	HS or Less	29-17-1-51
*Den: Ath/Agn	44-8-0-48	35-44	41-16-3-36
Den: Cath	43-12-1-41	South	39-14-3-42
Den: None	43-11-3-43	Rsd: Cath	38-14-2-44
65+	43-22-2-34	Dems	46-14-2-35
Exec: 10-15 Yrs	43-6-1-50	Midwest	35-14-2-50
Neither Con/Lib	43-13-4-39	Den: Bapt	34-14-5-45
Exec: 25+ Yrs	43-11-2-41	Independents	40-13-2-43
Coll Grad	42-10-3-41	Born-Agn: Yes	41-13-1-43
Women	42-10-2-43	Men	39-13-3-44
Emply: 101-250	42-26-6-26	Very Cons	35-13-1-49
Liberal	42-13-2-41	Neither Con/Lib	43-13-4-39

Question 15
Noticed Legal, Yet Unethical Actions/Mention to Coworker? (part 2*)

1. Yes/Usually Mention: 40
2. Yes/Usually Keep Quiet: 12
3. Yes/No Opinion: 3
4. No: 43
5. Refused: 2

* Note: Crosstabs below are for categories 3 and 4. Categories 1 and 2 are on the previous page.

Yes/No Opinion		No	
Rsd: No Rel	54-7-2-37	*Den: Non-Chr	27-27-0-40
West	50-9-5-36	Emply: 101-250	42-26-6-26
Den: Presb	25-19-13-41	Rsd: Luth	33-5-3-60
Rsd: Presb	32-18-9-38	55-64	34-7-3-56
Emply: 101-250	42-26-6-26	*Den: Meth	37-7-0-56
Post-Grad Deg	40-11-6-43	Emply: 4-10	35-7-1-55
West	50-9-5-36	Rsd: Meth	37-10-0-54
Den: Bapt	34-14-5-45	HS or Less	29-17-1-51
Born-Agn: No	37-12-4-44	*Den: Luth	36-7-4-50
Emply: 250+	49-19-4-28	Midwest	35-14-2-50
Neither Con/Lib	43-13-4-39	Rsd: Bapt	33-13-1-50
*Den: Luth	36-7-4-50	Exec: 10-15 Yrs	43-6-1-50
35-44	41-16-3-36	Very Cons	35-13-1-49
Exec: <5 Yrs	36-17-3-39	*Den: Ath/Agn	44-8-0-48
Coll Grad	42-10-3-41	Exec: 15-25 Yrs	41-9-3-47
Exec: 15-25 Yrs	41-9-3-47	Northeast	39-9-0-47
Rsd: Oth Chr	48-12-3-35	Repblcns	39-11-3-46
South	39-14-3-42	Den: Bapt	34-14-5-45
Repblcns	39-11-3-46	Emply: 26-100	38-12-3-45
Den: None	43-11-3-43	Smwt Cons	40-10-3-45
Emply: 11-25	44-11-3-38	Born-Agn: No	37-12-4-44
55-64	34-7-3-56	18-34	41-13-2-44

Question 16
Role Played by Religious/Spiritual Beliefs In Turning Points (part 1*)

1. Major Role: 49
2. Moderate Role: 26
3. Minor Role: 14
4. No Role At All: 11
5. No Opinion: 1

* Note: Crosstabs below are for categories 1 and 2. Categories 3 and 4 are on the next page.

Major Role		Moderate Role	
Born-Agn: Yes	77-19-4-0	*Den: Meth	44-44-7-4
Den: Oth Chr	75-14-9-2	Rsd: Meth	33-40-13-12
Den: Bapt	66-30-5-0	Rsd: Luth	38-38-8-18
Very Cons	66-19-8-7	*Rsd: Non-Chr	19-38-13-31
Rsd: Oth Chr	64-18-11-7	*Den: Luth	50-36-11-4
Rsd: Bapt	63-26-6-6	*Den: Non-Chr	27-33-20-20
45-54	58-22-11-8	Liberal	30-33-18-17
Exec: 15-25 Yrs	56-20-10-10	Born-Agn: No	47-33-16-4
Smwt Cons	55-24-14-6	Emply: 26-100	46-33-13-8
Post-Grad Deg	55-26-10-9	Dems	41-32-15-11
Emply: 4-10	54-23-13-9	Emply: 101-250	39-32-10-19
West	54-20-13-14	Den: Presb	50-31-16-3
Den: Cath	53-31-14-1	Den: Cath	53-31-14-1
Repblcns	53-25-14-9	Exec: 5-10 Yrs	45-31-12-12
Exec: 10-15 Yrs	53-24-18-6	Neither Con/Lib	40-30-14-15
Women	53-27-10-9	35-44	43-30-17-10
55-64	51-25-13-9	Den: Bapt	66-30-5-0
Rsd: Cath	51-26-15-7	65+	51-29-9-11
HS or Less	51-25-8-14	South	48-29-13-8
65+	51-29-9-11	Some Coll/Voc	50-28-13-7

Question 16
Role Played by Religious/Spiritual Beliefs In Turning Points (part 2*)

1. Major Role: 49
2. Moderate Role: 26
3. Minor Role: 14
4. No Role At All: 11
5. No Opinion: 1

* Note: Crosstabs below are for categories 3 and 4. Categories 1 and 2 are on the previous page.

Minor Role		No Role at All	
Rsd: Presb	41-26-26-6	*Den: Ath/Agn	12-24-16-48
Coll Grad	42-25-20-13	*Rsd: Non-Chr	19-38-13-31
*Den: Non-Chr	27-33-20-20	Rsd: No Rel	37-15-17-28
Den: None	26-28-18-27	Den: None	26-28-18-27
Exec: 10-15 Yrs	53-24-18-6	*Den: Non-Chr	27-33-20-20
Liberal	30-33-18-17	Emply: 101-250	39-32-10-19
Rsd: No Rel	37-15-17-28	Rsd: Luth	38-38-8-18
Northeast	41-27-17-14	Liberal	30-33-18-17
35-44	43-30-17-10	18-34	42-26-16-16
Emply: 250+	43-28-16-11	Neither Con/Lib	40-30-14-15
18-34	42-26-16-16	HS or Less	51-25-8-14
Born-Agn: No	47-33-16-4	West	54-20-13-14
*Den: Ath/Agn	12-24-16-48	Northeast	41-27-17-14
Exec: <5 Yrs	45-27-16-12	Independents	48-22-13-13
Den: Presb	50-31-16-3	Coll Grad	42-25-20-13
Men	46-25-16-12	Emply: 11-25	47-26-13-13
Dems	41-32-15-11	Exec: 25+ Yrs	50-27-11-12
Rsd: Cath	51-26-15-7	Men	46-25-16-12
Den: Cath	53-31-14-1	Exec: 5-10 Yrs	45-31-12-12
Neither Con/Lib	40-30-14-15	Exec: <5 Yrs	45-27-16-12

Question 17
Religious Beliefs (part 1*)

1. Religious: 53
2. Spiritual But Not Religious: 36
3. Neither: 9
4. No Opinion: 2

* Note: Crosstabs below are for categories 1 and 2. Categories 3 and 4 are on the next page.

Religious		**Spiritual But Not Religious**	
Den: Bapt	82-16-2-0	Den: None	20-61-18-1
Born-Agn: Yes	79-19-1-0	Liberal	34-51-14-1
Den: Presb	72-25-0-3	*Den: Ath/Agn	8-48-44-0
*Den: Meth	70-26-4-0	Emply: 26-100	42-46-9-3
Very Cons	70-26-3-1	Emply: 101-250	42-45-13-0
Den: Cath	67-29-3-1	Independents	44-44-12-0
Den: Oth Chr	66-30-3-1	West	45-43-12-0
Rsd: Bapt	66-33-1-0	45-54	53-42-4-1
Rsd: Presb	62-32-3-3	Rsd: No Rel	33-41-24-2
Born-Agn: No	62-33-5-1	Post-Grad Deg	50-41-7-2
65+	62-29-6-3	Neither Con/Lib	48-40-11-1
Midwest	61-30-8-1	Rsd: Cath	53-40-5-1
*Den: Luth	61-29-7-4	*Den: Non-Chr	40-40-20-0
Repblcns	60-31-8-2	Dems	48-39-12-1
Exec: 10-15 Yrs	60-28-10-3	Exec: <5 Yrs	51-39-9-1
Smwt Cons	60-29-10-2	35-44	50-38-11-1
Emply: 4-10	58-33-8-1	*Rsd: Non-Chr	31-38-31-0
Exec: 15-25 Yrs	57-34-6-2	Women	55-37-7-1
18-34	57-30-13-0	Exec: 25+ Yrs	52-37-10-1
Emply: 250+	56-34-10-0	South	54-36-9-1
Emply: 11-25	55-32-11-3	South	54-36-9-1

Question 17
Religious Beliefs (part 2*)

1. Religious: 53
2. Spiritual But Not Religious: 36
3. Neither: 9
4. No Opinion: 2

* Note: Crosstabs below are for categories 3 and 4. Categories 1 and 2 are on the previous page.

Neither		**No Opinion**	
*Den: Ath/Agn	8-48-44-0	Rsd: Luth	55-28-13-5
*Rsd: Non-Chr	31-38-31-0	Northeast	52-34-9-5
Rsd: No Rel	33-41-24-2	*Den: Luth	61-29-7-4
*Den: Non-Chr	40-40-20-0	Den: Presb	72-25-0-3
Den: None	20-61-18-1	65+	62-29-6-3
Liberal	34-51-14-1	Rsd: Presb	62-32-3-3
Rsd: Meth	54-33-13-0	Emply: 11-25	55-32-11-3
55-64	51-34-13-2	Exec: 10-15 Yrs	60-28-10-3
Emply: 101-250	42-45-13-0	Emply: 26-100	42-46-9-3
18-34	57-30-13-0	Post-Grad Deg	50-41-7-2
Exec: 5-10 Yrs	50-36-13-1	Rsd: No Rel	33-41-24-2
Rsd: Luth	55-28-13-5	Exec: 15-25 Yrs	57-34-6-2
Coll Grad	54-33-12-1	Some Coll/Voc	54-36-9-2
Dems	48-39-12-1	55-64	51-34-13-2
West	45-43-12-0	Repblcns	60-31-8-2
Independents	44-44-12-0	Smwt Cons	60-29-10-2
Men	53-35-11-1	Women	55-37-7-1
35-44	50-38-11-1	Aggregate	54-36-9-1
Neither Con/Lib	48-40-11-1	Men	53-35-11-1
Emply: 11-25	55-32-11-3	South	54-36-9-1

Question 18
Serious Talk With Religious Leader: Theological Issues/Questions

1. Yes: 44
2. No: 55
3. Refused: 1

Yes		**No**		**Refused**	
Born-Agn: Yes	64-36-1	*Den: Ath/Agn	12-84-4	*Rsd: Non-Chr	19-75-6
Den: Presb	63-38-0	*Rsd: Non-Chr	19-75-6	*Den: Ath/Agn	12-84-4
Den: Oth Chr	61-38-1	*Den: Meth	30-70-0	Rsd: Bapt	49-49-3
Post-Grad Deg	55-45-0	Den: None	30-70-0	Den: Bapt	52-45-2
Rsd: Presb	53-47-0	Rsd: No Rel	30-70-0	Northeast	48-50-2
Den: Bapt	52-45-2	Rsd: Meth	33-67-0	Exec: <5 Yrs	45-53-2
Very Cons	51-48-1	*Den: Non-Chr	33-67-0	HS or Less	32-66-2
Rsd: Luth	50-50-0	HS or Less	32-66-2	Emply: 11-25	48-50-2
*Den: Luth	50-50-0	Liberal	34-65-1	65+	42-57-2
Some Coll/Voc	49-51-0	Emply: 101-250	39-61-0	Women	41-57-1
Rsd: Bapt	49-49-3	Exec: 5-10 Yrs	40-59-1	Emply: 26-100	47-51-1
Emply: 11-25	48-50-2	Coll Grad	40-59-1	Coll Grad	40-59-1
35-44	48-51-1	Midwest	42-58-0	South	43-56-1
Northeast	48-50-2	Emply: 250+	42-58-0	Neither Con/Lib	44-55-1
Repblcns	48-52-0	Born-Agn: No	42-58-0	18-34	42-57-1
Emply: 26-100	47-51-1	Emply: 4-10	42-58-0	Very Cons	51-48-1
Rsd: Cath	47-53-0	Women	41-57-1	Exec: 5-10 Yrs	40-59-1
Smwt Cons	46-53-1	Dems	42-57-1	Den: Oth Chr	61-38-1
Exec: 10-15 Yrs	46-54-0	55-64	43-57-0	35-44	48-51-1
Men	46-54-0	18-34	42-57-1	Dems	42-57-1

Question 19:
Serious Talk With Religious Leader: Personal/Marital/Family

1. Yes: 33
2. No: 66
3. Refused: 0

Yes		No		Refused	
Born-Agn: Yes	49-51-0	*Den: Ath/Agn	12-84-4	*Rsd: Non-Chr	13-81-6
Den: Oth Chr	48-52-0	Den: None	18-82-0	*Den: Ath/Agn	12-84-4
18-34	47-52-1	*Rsd: Non-Chr	13-81-6	Northeast	31-67-2
Den: Bapt	45-55-0	*Den: Non-Chr	20-80-0	Exec: <5 Yrs	37-62-1
Emply: 11-25	41-58-1	Exec: 25+ Yrs	22-78-0	Emply: 26-100	38-61-1
Den: Presb	41-59-0	65+	25-75-0	Coll Grad	31-68-1
Rsd: Bapt	40-60-0	Rsd: Luth	25-75-0	Neither Con/Lib	35-64-1
Smwt Cons	40-60-0	Rsd: Meth	25-75-0	18-34	47-52-1
Some Coll/Voc	38-62-0	Liberal	25-74-1	Emply: 11-25	41-58-1
Emply: 26-100	38-61-1	Emply: 101-250	26-74-0	Liberal	25-74-1
Exec: 5-10 Yrs	38-62-0	55-64	26-74-0	Women	35-65-0
35-44	37-63-0	Exec: 10-15 Yrs	28-72-0	Repblcns	37-63-0
Rsd: Oth Chr	37-63-0	Independents	28-72-0	Aggregate	33-66-0
Exec: <5 Yrs	37-62-1	Emply: 4-10	29-71-0	Men	33-67-0
Repblcns	37-63-0	Post-Grad Deg	31-69-0	Exec: 15-25 Yrs	36-64-0
Exec: 15-25 Yrs	36-64-0	Very Cons	31-69-0	Emply: 250+	34-66-0
*Den: Luth	36-64-0	Born-Agn: No	31-69-0	Born-Agn: No	31-69-0
Midwest	36-64-0	Coll Grad	31-68-1	Emply: 101-250	26-74-0
Rsd: Presb	35-65-0	HS or Less	32-68-0	Exec: 10-15 Yrs	28-72-0
Women	35-65-0	South	33-67-0	Emply: 4-10	29-71-0

Question 20
Serious Talk With Religious Leader: Business Problems

1. Yes: 19
2. No: 81
3. Refused: 0

Yes		No		Refused	
Den: Presb	38-63-0	*Den: Non-Chr	7-93-0	*Rsd: Non-Chr	6-88-6
Den: Oth Chr	34-66-0	*Den: Luth	7-93-0	*Den: Ath/Agn	4-92-4
Den: Bapt	32-68-0	*Den: Ath/Agn	4-92-4	Northeast	13-85-2
Born-Agn: Yes	31-69-0	*Den: Meth	11-89-0	Exec: <5 Yrs	14-85-1
Very Cons	28-72-0	Den: Cath	11-89-0	Emply: 26-100	28-71-1
Rsd: Oth Chr	28-72-0	Emply: 250+	11-89-0	Coll Grad	18-81-1
Emply: 26-100	28-71-1	Rsd: Meth	12-88-0	Neither Con/Lib	13-86-1
Rsd: Presb	26-74-0	Den: None	12-88-0	18-34	19-80-1
Exec: 5-10 Yrs	25-75-0	*Rsd: Non-Chr	6-88-6	Emply: 11-25	16-83-1
Exec: 15-25 Yrs	24-76-0	Rsd: Luth	13-88-0	Liberal	15-85-1
Post-Grad Deg	24-76-0	55-64	14-86-0	Women	20-80-0
35-44	23-77-0	Neither Con/Lib	13-86-1	Repblcns	21-79-0
Rsd: Bapt	23-77-0	Independents	14-86-0	Aggregate	19-81-0
Midwest	23-77-0	Northeast	13-85-2	Men	18-81-0
Repblcns	21-79-0	Exec: <5 Yrs	14-85-1	Exec: 15-25 Yrs	24-76-0
45-54	21-79-0	Exec: 10-15 Yrs	15-85-0	Emply: 250+	11-89-0
Emply: 4-10	21-79-0	Liberal	15-85-1	Born-Agn: No	17-83-0
West	21-79-0	HS or Less	16-84-0	Emply: 101-250	19-81-0
Women	20-80-0	Born-Agn: No	17-83-0	Exec: 10-15 Yrs	15-85-0
Some Coll/Voc	20-80-0	Rsd: Cath	17-83-0	Emply: 4-10	21-79-0

Question 21
Serious Talk With Religious Leader: Career/Employment Decisions

1. Yes: 17
2. No: 83
3. Refused: 0

Yes		**No**		**Refused**	
Den: Oth Chr	31-69-0	*Den: Meth	4-96-0	*Rsd: Non-Chr	6-88-6
Emply: 101-250	29-71-0	Den: None	8-92-0	*Den: Ath/Agn	4-92-4
Den: Presb	28-72-0	65+	8-92-0	Northeast	14-84-2
Den: Bapt	27-73-0	*Den: Ath/Agn	4-92-4	Exec: <5 Yrs	18-81-1
Born-Agn: Yes	26-74-0	Emply: 250+	9-91-0	Emply: 26-100	22-76-1
Post-Grad Deg	25-75-0	Exec: 25+ Yrs	10-90-0	Coll Grad	12-86-1
Rsd: Presb	24-76-0	Rsd: Meth	12-88-0	Neither Con/Lib	14-85-1
Emply: 26-100	22-76-1	Den: Cath	12-88-0	18-34	20-79-1
Exec: 5-10 Yrs	22-78-0	Exec: 10-15 Yrs	13-88-0	Emply: 11-25	15-84-1
Very Cons	22-78-0	*Rsd: Non-Chr	6-88-6	Liberal	15-85-1
35-44	22-78-0	HS or Less	13-87-0	Women	17-82-0
Rsd: Oth Chr	22-78-0	Dems	13-87-0	Repblcns	20-80-0
Rsd: Bapt	21-79-0	Rsd: No Rel	13-87-0	Aggregate	17-83-0
Some Coll/Voc	20-80-0	55-64	13-87-0	Men	17-83-0
45-54	20-80-0	*Den: Non-Chr	13-87-0	Exec: 15-25 Yrs	20-80-0
Exec: 15-25 Yrs	20-80-0	Independents	13-87-0	Emply: 250+	9-91-0
18-34	20-79-1	Coll Grad	12-86-1	Born-Agn: No	16-84-0
Midwest	20-80-0	Liberal	15-85-1	Emply: 101-250	29-71-0
Repblcns	20-80-0	Neither Con/Lib	14-85-1	Exec: 10-15 Yrs	13-88-0
*Den: Luth	18-82-0	Northeast	14-84-2	Emply: 4-10	17-83-0

Question 22
Have You Prayed at Work by Yourself?

1. Yes: 72
2. No: 27
3. No Opinion/Refused: 0

Yes		No		Refused	
Born-Agn: Yes	96-4-0	*Den: Non-Chr	33-67-0	Exec: 10-15 Yrs	75-24-1
Den: Bapt	95-5-0	*Den: Ath/Agn	36-64-0	Emply: 26-100	68-30-1
Rsd: Bapt	86-14-0	*Rsd: Non-Chr	38-63-0	Coll Grad	62-36-1
*Den: Meth	85-15-0	Liberal	56-44-1	Emply: 250+	72-27-1
Very Cons	83-16-1	Rsd: No Rel	57-43-0	Northeast	61-38-1
*Den: Luth	82-18-0	Den: None	60-40-0	Den: Cath	73-26-1
45-54	82-18-0	18-34	62-38-0	Very Cons	83-16-1
Den: Oth Chr	82-18-0	Northeast	61-38-1	Women	75-24-1
Den: Presb	81-19-0	Emply: 11-25	63-38-0	35-44	69-30-1
Smwt Cons	81-19-0	Coll Grad	62-36-1	Liberal	56-44-1
65+	80-20-0	Neither Con/Lib	65-35-0	West	68-31-1
Some Coll/Voc	79-21-0	Dems	68-32-0	Rsd: Cath	74-25-1
Emply: 4-10	78-22-0	West	68-31-1	Exec: <5 Yrs	71-29-1
South	78-22-0	35-44	69-30-1	Born-Agn: No	70-29-1
Rsd: Presb	76-24-0	Emply: 26-100	68-30-1	Repblcns	76-23-0
Repblcns	76-23-0	55-64	70-30-0	Aggregate	72-27-0
Midwest	76-24-0	Men	70-30-0	Emply: 101-250	71-29-0
Rsd: Luth	75-25-0	Exec: 25+ Yrs	71-29-0	Emply: 11-25	63-38-0
Exec: 10-15 Yrs	75-24-1	Emply: 101-250	71-29-0	Emply: 4-10	78-22-0
Women	75-24-1	Born-Agn: No	70-29-1	Exec: 15-25 Yrs	74-26-0

Question 23
Have You Prayed at Work With Others?

1. Yes: 30
2. No: 69
3. No Opinion/Refused: 1

Yes		**No**		**Refused**	
Born-Agn: Yes	54-46-0	*Rsd: Non-Chr	0-**-0	*Den: Luth	32-64-4
Den: Bapt	43-57-0	*Den: Non-Chr	0-**-0	Emply: 101-250	32-65-3
65+	42-57-2	*Den: Ath/Agn	8-92-0	Post-Grad Deg	34-64-2
Den: Oth Chr	41-59-0	Northeast	18-81-1	Independents	32-66-2
Den: Presb	41-59-0	Born-Agn: No	20-79-1	65+	42-57-2
Very Cons	40-60-0	Den: None	20-79-1	Rsd: Bapt	39-60-1
South	39-60-1	18-34	22-78-0	Exec: <5 Yrs	23-75-1
Rsd: Bapt	39-60-1	Liberal	21-78-1	Emply: 26-100	29-70-1
Rsd: Presb	38-62-0	*Den: Meth	22-78-0	Emply: 250+	30-68-1
Exec: 10-15 Yrs	38-63-0	Rsd: Meth	23-77-0	Neither Con/Lib	23-76-1
Exec: 15-25 Yrs	36-64-0	Neither Con/Lib	23-76-1	Northeast	18-81-1
Women	34-65-0	Exec: <5 Yrs	23-75-1	Exec: 5-10 Yrs	27-72-1
Post-Grad Deg	34-64-2	Coll Grad	24-75-1	Den: None	20-79-1
Rsd: Oth Chr	34-66-0	Rsd: Luth	25-75-0	35-44	28-71-1
45-54	34-66-0	Emply: 11-25	25-75-0	Liberal	21-78-1
Repblcns	33-67-0	West	26-74-0	Rsd: Cath	31-69-1
HS or Less	32-68-0	Den: Cath	27-73-0	Midwest	30-70-1
Smwt Cons	32-67-1	Dems	27-73-0	Men	27-72-1
Emply: 101-250	32-65-3	Men	27-72-1	Coll Grad	24-75-1
*Den: Luth	32-64-4	Exec: 5-10 Yrs	27-72-1	Born-Agn: No	20-79-1

Question 24
Have You Counseled an Employee/Associate at Work?

1. Yes: 76
2. No: 24
3. No Opinion/Refused: 1

Yes		No		No Opinion/Refused	
Emply: 101-250	84-16-0	*Den: Non-Chr	53-47-0	*Den: Meth	63-33-4
Den: Cath	83-17-0	*Rsd: Non-Chr	56-44-0	*Den: Luth	71-25-4
Neither Con/Lib	82-18-0	*Den: Ath/Agn	64-36-0	Northeast	77-19-3
45-54	82-17-1	Independents	63-36-1	Exec: 25+ Yrs	74-23-2
Post-Grad Deg	82-17-1	*Den: Meth	63-33-4	Liberal	76-22-2
Den: Oth Chr	82-18-0	Rsd: Meth	67-33-0	65+	71-28-2
Exec: 5-10 Yrs	82-18-0	HS or Less	70-30-0	Born-Agn: Yes	81-18-1
Rsd: Cath	81-18-1	18-34	71-29-0	Rsd: Bapt	77-21-1
Born-Agn: Yes	81-18-1	Rsd: No Rel	72-28-0	Some Coll/Voc	77-21-1
Repblcns	80-19-1	Exec: <5 Yrs	71-28-1	Emply: 26-100	74-25-1
Den: Bapt	80-20-0	65+	71-28-2	Emply: 250+	77-22-1
Rsd: Presb	79-21-0	Rsd: Luth	73-28-0	Post-Grad Deg	82-17-1
35-44	79-21-0	Women	72-27-0	Exec: 15-25 Yrs	77-22-1
Dems	79-21-0	Smwt Cons	72-27-1	Men	78-21-1
Men	78-21-1	Den: None	74-26-0	Rsd: Oth Chr	76-23-1
West	78-22-0	Midwest	74-26-0	Very Cons	78-21-1
Very Cons	78-21-1	Coll Grad	74-25-1	Independents	63-36-1
Some Coll/Voc	77-21-1	55-64	74-25-1	55-64	74-25-1
Northeast	77-19-3	South	74-25-1	45-54	82-17-1
Emply: 250+	77-22-1	Den: Presb	75-25-0	Repblcns	80-19-1

Question 25
Have You Discussed Religion With Employees at Your Workplace?

1. Yes: 59
2. No: 40
3. No Opinion/Refused: 1

Yes		No		No Opinion/Refused	
Den: Oth Chr	78-22-0	*Den: Non-Chr	27-73-0	Emply: 26-100	61-38-1
Den: Bapt	77-23-0	*Rsd: Non-Chr	31-69-0	Emply: 250+	56-43-1
Born-Agn: Yes	77-22-1	*Den: Ath/Agn	36-64-0	Northeast	47-52-1
Rsd: Oth Chr	74-26-0	55-64	45-55-0	Den: Cath	49-50-1
Rsd: Bapt	71-29-0	Rsd: No Rel	46-54-0	Exec: 15-25 Yrs	63-36-1
Post-Grad Deg	68-32-0	Northeast	47-52-1	Exec: 5-10 Yrs	56-43-1
45-54	68-32-0	Coll Grad	48-51-1	Emply: 11-25	54-45-1
Some Coll/Voc	66-34-1	Rsd: Luth	50-50-0	35-44	59-40-1
65+	65-35-0	Den: Cath	49-50-1	Liberal	50-49-1
Emply: 101-250	65-35-0	Born-Agn: No	50-50-0	Dems	56-43-1
South	64-35-1	Liberal	50-49-1	West	63-36-1
Neither Con/Lib	64-36-0	Den: None	53-47-0	Rsd: Cath	57-42-1
Exec: <5 Yrs	64-36-1	*Den: Luth	54-46-0	Born-Agn: Yes	77-22-1
Very Cons	64-36-0	Rsd: Meth	54-46-0	Men	60-39-1
West	63-36-1	Exec: 10-15 Yrs	54-46-0	Exec: <5 Yrs	64-36-1
18-34	63-37-0	Emply: 11-25	54-45-1	Some Coll/Voc	66-34-1
Den: Presb	63-38-0	Exec: 25+ Yrs	55-45-0	Coll Grad	48-51-1
Exec: 15-25 Yrs	63-36-1	*Den: Meth	56-44-0	South	64-35-1
Repblcns	62-38-0	Rsd: Presb	56-44-0	Aggregate	59-40-1
Emply: 4-10	61-39-0	Emply: 250+	56-43-1	Smwt Cons	60-39-1

Question 26
Have You Discussed Religion With Employees Outside of Your Workplace?

1. Yes: 55
2. No: 45
3. No Opinion/Refused: 0

Yes		No		No Opinion/Refused	
Den: Oth Chr	74-26-0	*Den: Non-Chr	33-67-0	Emply: 26-100	47-50-3
Born-Agn: Yes	72-28-0	*Den: Ath/Agn	36-64-0	Rsd: Luth	55-43-3
Rsd: Presb	71-29-0	*Rsd: Non-Chr	38-63-0	Northeast	52-45-2
Den: Bapt	66-34-0	Rsd: No Rel	43-57-0	Liberal	55-44-2
Den: Presb	66-34-0	Rsd: Meth	44-56-0	Coll Grad	47-51-1
Post-Grad Deg	64-36-0	Den: Cath	44-56-0	18-34	56-43-1
Rsd: Oth Chr	63-37-0	Den: None	44-55-1	Exec: 5-10 Yrs	46-53-1
Rsd: Bapt	63-37-0	Exec: 5-10 Yrs	46-53-1	Independents	53-46-1
Emply: 101-250	61-39-0	Born-Agn: No	47-53-0	Den: None	44-55-1
Emply: 250+	59-41-0	55-64	48-52-0	Exec: <5 Yrs	58-41-1
Dems	59-41-0	*Den: Meth	48-52-0	Women	57-43-0
65+	58-42-0	Coll Grad	47-51-1	Aggregate	55-45-0
Exec: 15-25 Yrs	58-42-0	*Den: Luth	50-50-0	Men	53-46-0
Exec: <5 Yrs	58-41-1	Emply: 26-100	47-50-3	Repblcns	56-44-0
Women	57-43-0	Rsd: Cath	50-50-0	Emply: 250+	59-41-0
HS or Less	57-43-0	Neither Con/Lib	52-48-0	Born-Agn: No	47-53-0
35-44	57-43-0	Men	53-46-0	Exec: 15-25 Yrs	58-42-0
South	56-44-0	West	54-46-0	Emply: 101-250	61-39-0
Exec: 25+ Yrs	56-44-0	Independents	53-46-1	Born-Agn: Yes	72-28-0
45-54	56-44-0	Emply: 11-25	54-46-0	Midwest	55-45-0

Question 27: Have You Attended a Worship Service of a Denomination Other Than Your Own?

1. Yes: 81
2. No: 19
3. No Opinion/Refused: 1

Yes		No		No Opinion/Refused	
Rsd: Luth	93-8-0	*Den: Non-Chr	67-33-0	Emply: 26-100	72-25-3
Post-Grad Deg	91-9-0	*Den: Ath/Agn	68-32-0	Den: Bapt	75-23-2
Den: Presb	91-9-0	Rsd: No Rel	70-30-0	Rsd: Bapt	70-29-1
*Den: Luth	89-11-0	18-34	70-29-1	Exec: <5 Yrs	75-24-1
*Den: Meth	89-11-0	Emply: 101-250	71-29-0	18-34	70-29-1
Rsd: Presb	88-12-0	Rsd: Bapt	70-29-1	Northeast	82-17-1
Exec: 15-25 Yrs	86-14-0	HS or Less	71-28-1	Smwt Cons	81-18-1
Very Cons	86-14-0	Liberal	73-26-1	Rsd: Oth Chr	81-18-1
Repblcns	86-14-0	Den: None	74-26-0	HS or Less	71-28-1
Born-Agn: Yes	85-15-0	Emply: 26-100	72-25-3	Exec: 5-10 Yrs	83-17-1
55-64	84-16-0	*Rsd: Non-Chr	75-25-0	Emply: 11-25	81-18-1
South	84-15-1	West	74-25-1	Den: Oth Chr	83-16-1
Den: Cath	83-17-0	Exec: <5 Yrs	75-24-1	Independents	79-20-1
Emply: 4-10	83-17-0	Den: Bapt	75-23-2	Women	82-17-1
Rsd: Cath	83-17-0	Exec: 10-15 Yrs	78-22-0	35-44	81-18-1
65+	83-17-0	Dems	78-21-1	West	74-25-1
Exec: 25+ Yrs	83-17-0	Men	79-21-0	Liberal	73-26-1
45-54	83-17-0	Independents	79-20-1	Dems	78-21-1
Den: Oth Chr	83-16-1	Some Coll/Voc	79-20-1	Some Coll/Voc	79-20-1
Exec: 5-10 Yrs	83-17-1	Midwest	80-20-0	Coll Grad	81-18-1

Question 28
Have You Investigated Another Religion With Thought of Joining?

1. Yes: 26
2. No: 74
3. No Opinion/Refused: 0

Yes		No		No Opinion/Refused	
Den: None	39-61-0	*Rsd: Non-Chr	13-88-0	*Den: Luth	29-68-4
Rsd: Presb	38-62-0	*Den: Meth	15-85-0	Rsd: Luth	23-75-3
45-54	34-66-0	Den: Bapt	16-84-0	Emply: 26-100	20-79-1
Liberal	32-68-0	*Den: Ath/Agn	16-84-0	Post-Grad Deg	25-74-1
35-44	30-70-0	Exec: 25+ Yrs	18-82-0	Exec: 15-25 Yrs	24-75-1
Neither Con/Lib	30-70-0	65+	18-82-0	55-64	21-79-1
Exec: <5 Yrs	29-71-0	Born-Agn: Yes	21-79-0	Midwest	24-75-1
Some Coll/Voc	29-71-0	Born-Agn: No	21-79-0	Smwt Cons	21-78-1
Dems	29-71-0	Emply: 26-100	20-79-1	Women	28-72-0
Emply: 4-10	29-71-0	55-64	21-79-1	Repblcns	24-76-0
*Den: Luth	29-68-4	Smwt Cons	21-78-1	Aggregate	26-74-0
Northeast	28-72-0	HS or Less	22-78-0	Emply: 4-10	29-71-0
Rsd: Cath	28-72-0	Rsd: No Rel	22-78-0	Born-Agn: No	21-79-0
West	28-72-0	18-34	22-78-0	Exec: <5 Yrs	29-71-0
Women	28-72-0	Den: Cath	22-78-0	Exec: 10-15 Yrs	26-74-0
Independents	28-72-0	Emply: 101-250	23-77-0	Independents	28-72-0
Emply: 250+	28-72-0	South	24-76-0	Men	24-76-0
Exec: 5-10 Yrs	27-73-0	Emply: 11-25	24-76-0	Exec: 5-10 Yrs	27-73-0
*Den: Non-Chr	27-73-0	Men	24-76-0	West	28-72-0
Exec: 10-15 Yrs	26-74-0	Repblcns	24-76-0	Emply: 101-250	23-77-0

Question 29
Frequency: Read Religious Book at Work During Breaks/Lunch (part 1*)

1. Yes/Daily: 9
2. Yes/2-3 Times a Week: 7
3. Yes/Weekly: 3
4. Yes/2-3 Times a Month: 2
5. Yes/Monthly: 2
6. Yes/Less Often Than Monthly: 7
7. Yes/No Opinion/Refused: 2
8. No, No Relious Book at Work: 69
9. Refused: 0

* Note: Crosstabs below are for categories 1, 2, 3. Categories 4,5, and 6 are on the next page. Categories 7 and 8 are on the page following.

Yes/Daily		Yes/2-3 Times a Week		Yes/Weekly	
Den: Pres	22-3-6-0	*Den: Luth	0-14-0-0	Den: Bapt	18-9-9-2
Born-Agn: Yes	20-11-7-3	Den: Oth Chr	15-12-5-3	Born-Agn: Yes	20-11-7-3
Very Cons	19-5-5-3	Born-Agn: Yes	20-11-7-3	Rsd: Oth Chr	13-4-7-2
Den: Bapt	18-9-9-2	Exec: 25+ Yrs	11-11-6-1	Den: Pres	22-3-6-0
Rsd: Bapt	16-10-4-1	Emply: 11-25	9-11-4-0	65+	12-8-6-3
Den: Oth Chr	15-12-5-3	Rsd: Luth	5-10-3-0	Exec: 25+ Yrs	11-11-6-1
Exec: 10-15 Yrs	14-7-0-0	Rsd: Bapt	16-10-4-1	Exec: 15-25 Yrs	11-5-5-2
Rsd: Oth Chr	13-4-7-2	South	11-10-4-2	Very Cons	19-5-5-3
Emply: 4-10	13-6-3-2	Rsd: Meth	2-10-0-6	Den: Oth Chr	15-12-5-3
55-64	13-7-3-1	Neither Con/Lib	5-10-1-1	Rsd: Bapt	16-10-4-1
Some Coll/Voc	13-7-1-2	Liberal	1-9-2-1	HS or Less	11-8-4-3
65+	12-8-6-3	Den: Bapt	18-9-9-2	Coll Grad	3-6-4-2
Midwest	12-8-2-1	Rsd: No Rel	9-9-0-0	Emply: 11-25	9-11-4-0
Rsd: Pres	12-0-3-0	Midwest	12-8-2-1	South	11-10-4-2
Repblcns	11-8-3-2	Repblcns	11-8-3-2	Emply: 4-10	13-6-3-2
Exec: 15-25 Yrs	11-5-5-2	HS or Less	11-8-4-3	West	7-4-3-3
Post-Grad Deg	11-7-2-2	65+	12-8-6-3	Repblcns	11-8-3-2
South	11-10-4-2	Women	9-8-3-3	Emply: 101-250	0-0-3-3
Exec: 25+ Yrs	11-11-6-1	Exec: <5 Yrs	3-8-1-3	Rsd: Pres	12-0-3-0
HS or Less	11-8-4-3	*Den: Meth	7-7-0-4	Women	9-8-3-3

Question 29
Frequency: Read Religious Book at Work During Breaks/Lunch (part 2*)

1. Yes/Daily: 9
2. Yes/2-3 Times a Week: 7
3. Yes/Weekly: 3
4. Yes/2-3 Times a Month: 2
5. Yes/Monthly: 2
6. Yes/Less Often Than Monthly: 7
7. Yes/No Opinion/Refused: 2
8. No, No Religious Book at Work: 69
9. Refused: 0

* Note: Crosstabs below are for categories 4,5, and 6. Categories 1-3 are on the previous page. Categories 7 and 8 are on the next page.

Yes/2-3 Times a Month		Yes/Monthly		Yes/Less Often Than Monthly	
Rsd: Meth	2-10-0-6	*Den: Meth	7-4-0-70	*Rsd: Non-Chr	0-13-0-88
Den: Cath	4-1-1-6	Den: Bapt	5-5-5-48	Exec: 15-25 Yrs	2-11-2-60
Emply: 26-100	9-5-0-5	Post-Grad Deg	5-7-1-65	18-34	2-10-0-71
Democrats	7-7-1-4	Born-Agn: Yes	4-7-1-46	Den: Cath	1-10-1-76
Exec: 5-10Yrs	10-4-2-4	Exec: 10-15Yrs	4-7-3-65	Midwest	1-10-2-64
Rsd: Cath	8-7-2-4	Rsd: Oth Chr	4-4-3-62	Emply: 101-250	0-10-3-81
*Den: Meth	7-7-0-4	HS or Less	4-5-3-63	Smwt Cons	1-9-2-66
18-34	5-7-1-3	South	4-7-3-59	Rsd: Bapt	3-9-3-54
35-44	7-7-3-3	Neither Con/Lib	4-2-2-75	Coll Grad	1-8-2-73
Northeast	3-2-1-3	*Den: Luth	4-7-0-75	55-64	1-8-5-63
Women	9-8-3-3	45-54	3-5-2-70	Emply: 26-100	3-8-0-70
Smwt Cons	11-5-3-3	Very Cons	3-5-2-58	Emply: 4-10	2-8-2-62
Emply: 101-250	0-0-3-3	Repblcns	3-6-1-65	Den: Oth Chr	2-8-2-54
Born-Agn: No	6-5-1-3	Rsd: Bapt	3-9-3-54	Independents	1-8-4-74
65+	12-8-6-3	Emply: 26-100	3-8-0-70	Rsd: Cath	1-8-2-70
Very Cons	19-5-5-3	Emply: 250+	3-6-1-78	Women	2-8-2-65
Born-Agn: Yes	20-11-7-3	Rsd: Luth	3-5-3-73	South	4-7-3-59
HS or Less	11-8-4-3	Exec: 25+ Yrs	2-2-1-65	*Den: Luth	4-7-0-75
Den: Oth Chr	15-12-5-3	Women	2-8-2-65	Exec: 10-15Yrs	4-7-3-65
Exec: <5 Yrs	3-8-1-3	18-34	2-10-0-71	Exec: <5 Yrs	1-7-2-75

Question 29
Frequency: Read Religious Book at Work During Breaks/Lunch (part 3*)

1. Yes/Daily: 9
2. Yes/2-3 Times a Week: 7
3. Yes/Weekly: 3
4. Yes/2-3 Times a Month: 2
5. Yes/Monthly: 2
6. Yes/Less Often Than Monthly: 7
7. Yes/No Opinion/Refused: 2
8. No/No Religious Book at Work: 69
9. Refused: 0

* Note: Crosstabs below are for categories 7 and 8. Categories 1-6 are on the predecing pages.

Yes/No Opinion/Refused	
55-64	1-8-5-63
Den: Bapt	5-5-5-48
Independents	1-8-4-74
Emply: 101-250	0-10-3-81
Rsd: Oth Chr	4-4-3-62
South	4-7-3-59
HS or Less	4-5-3-63
Rsd: Bapt	3-9-3-54
Exec: 10-15 Yrs	4-7-3-65
Rsd: Luth	3-5-3-73
Emply: 4-10	2-8-2-62
Neither Con/Lib	4-2-2-75
Midwest	1-10-2-64
Exec: 15-25 Yrs	2-11-2-60
Exec: <5 Yrs	1-7-2-75
Very Cons	3-5-2-58
Coll Grad	1-8-2-73
Den: None	1-6-2-81
Den: Oth Chr	2-8-2-54
Rsd: Meth	2-6-2-73

No/No Religious Book at Work	
*Den: Ath/Agn	0-4-0-88
*Rsd: Non-Chr	0-13-0-88
*Den: Non-Chr	0-7-0-87
Northeast	2-6-0-82
Den: None	1-6-2-81
Emply: 101-250	0-10-3-81
Rsd: Pres	0-6-0-79
West	1-3-1-79
Emply: 250+	3-6-1-78
Liberal	2-6-2-78
Born-Agn: No	1-7-1-77
Den: Cath	1-10-1-76
Neither Con/Lib	4-2-2-75
*Den: Luth	4-7-0-75
Exec: <5 Yrs	1-7-2-75
Independents	1-8-4-74
35-44	2-3-1-74
Rsd: No Rel	2-7-0-74
Exec: 5-10 Yrs	1-5-1-74
Democrats	2-4-2-74

Question 30
Member of a Church or Synagogue?

1. Yes: 72
2. No: 28
3. Refused: 0

Yes		No		Refused	
Den: Bapt	95-5-0	Den: None	32-68-0	Emply: 26-100	72-26-1
Born-Agn: Yes	93-7-0	*Den: Ath/Agn	32-68-0	Northeast	73-26-1
*Den: Luth	93-7-0	Rsd: No Rel	54-46-0	Liberal	56-43-1
*Den: Meth	93-7-0	Liberal	56-43-1	Exec: <5 Yrs	71-29-1
Den: Pres	88-13-0	Emply: 101-250	58-42-0	Coll Grad	69-30-1
Den: Oth Chr	88-13-0	Neither Con/Lib	62-38-0	Women	72-28-0
Den: Cath	87-13-0	West	62-38-0	Aggregate	72-28-0
Born-Agn: No	86-14-0	Democrats	64-36-0	Emply: 250+	72-28-0
Smwt Cons	82-18-0	Independents	66-34-0	Emply: 4-10	73-27-0
Repblcns	80-20-0	35-44	69-31-0	Exec: 15-25 Yrs	76-24-0
Rsd: Bapt	80-20-0	*Rsd: Non-Chr	69-31-0	Emply: 101-250	58-42-0
Very Cons	80-20-0	45-54	69-31-0	Born-Agn: Yes	93-7-0
55-64	79-21-0	Exec: 25+ Yrs	70-30-0	Born-Agn: No	86-14-0
Post-Grad Deg	77-23-0	HS or Less	70-30-0	Repblcns	80-20-0
Midwest	77-23-0	18-34	70-30-0	Exec: 5-10 Yrs	70-30-0
65+	77-23-0	Exec: 5-10 Yrs	70-30-0	Exec: 10-15 Yrs	75-25-0
Exec: 15-25 Yrs	76-24-0	Coll Grad	69-30-1	Men	72-28-0
Rsd: Luth	75-25-0	Rsd: Oth Chr	71-29-0	Emply: 11-25	72-28-0
Exec: 10-15 Yrs	75-25-0	Rsd: Meth	71-29-0	West	62-38-0
Rsd: Cath	75-25-0	Exec: <5 Yrs	71-29-1	Midwest	77-23-0

Question 31
Attend Religious Services Other Than Weddings/Funerals? (part 1*)

1. More Than Once A Week: 16
2. Once A Week: 31
3. Once Or Twice A Month: 17
4. A Few Times A Year: 15
5. Seldom: 15
6. Never: 6
7. No Opinion/Refused: 0

* Note: Crosstabs below are for categories 1-3. Categories 4-6 are on the next page.

More than Once/Week		Once a Week		Once or Twice/Month	
Den: Oth Chr	35-37-15	Born-Agn: Yes	30-50-14	Rsd: Pres	9-24-35
Den: Bapt	34-41-18	Den: Cath	6-47-19	*Den: Luth	18-39-29
Born-Agn: Yes	30-50-14	Den: Bapt	34-41-18	Den: Pres	9-38-28
Rsd: Bapt	27-36-11	*Den: Luth	18-39-29	*Den: Meth	11-37-26
Rsd: Oth Chr	26-31-12	Exec: 10-15 Yrs	11-39-14	18-34	16-24-24
Very Cons	25-37-19	45-54	13-38-13	Emply: 250+	11-30-24
South	23-31-12	Den: Pres	9-38-28	Born-Agn: No	11-34-23
65+	22-31-14	Very Cons	25-37-19	Midwest	17-33-21
Exec: 5-10 Yrs	21-22-17	*Den: Meth	11-37-26	Rsd: Meth	6-35-21
Smwt Cons	19-34-18	Rsd: Cath	14-37-15	Independents	10-30-21
Exec: 15-25 Yrs	19-33-14	Exec: 25+ Yrs	12-37-17	Rsd: Luth	15-30-20
Repblcns	18-33-17	Den: Oth Chr	35-37-15	Some Coll/Voc	17-32-20
Emply: 4-10	18-33-16	Rsd: Bapt	27-36-11	Exec: <5 Yrs	15-29-20
*Den: Luth	18-39-29	55-64	15-36-14	Rsd: No Rel	13-15-20
35-44	17-24-18	Rsd: Meth	6-35-21	Men	16-29-19
Emply: 11-25	17-27-15	Smwt Cons	19-34-18	Emply: 101-250	16-32-19
Some Coll/Voc	17-32-20	Born-Agn: No	11-34-23	Post-Grad Deg	16-28-19
HS or Less	17-32-9	Women	16-34-13	Very Cons	25-37-19
Midwest	17-33-21	Midwest	17-33-21	Den: Cath	6-47-19
18-34	16-24-24	Exec: 15-25 Yrs	19-33-14	35-44	17-24-18

Question 31
Frequency: Attend Religious Services Other Than Weddings/Funerals? (part 2*)

1. More Than Once A Week: 16
2. Once A Week: 31
3. Once Or Twice A Month: 17
4. A Few Times A Year: 15
5. Seldom: 15
6. Never: 6
7. No Opinion/Refused: 0

* Note: Crosstabs below are for categories 4, 5, and 6. Categories 1, 2, and 3 are on the next page.

Few Times a Year		Seldom		Never	
*Den: Non-Chr	40-20-7	Den: None	24-36-15	*Den: Ath/Agn	4-28-44
*Rsd: Non-Chr	31-31-13	*Rsd: Non-Chr	31-31-13	Rsd: No Rel	13-17-22
Emply: 26-100	25-14-5	*Den: Ath/Agn	4-28-44	Den: None	24-36-15
Den: None	24-36-15	Liberal	21-26-9	*Rsd: Non-Chr	31-31-13
Born-Agn: No	21-10-0	West	15-22-6	Neither Con/Lib	18-15-12
Exec: 10-15 Yrs	21-11-4	Rsd: Meth	13-21-4	HS or Less	16-16-11
Liberal	21-26-9	Emply: 250+	9-20-5	Emply: 101-250	13-10-10
Northeast	20-14-7	*Den: Non-Chr	40-20-7	Independents	16-13-10
Exec: 25+ Yrs	20-12-2	Exec: 5-10 Yrs	14-18-7	Liberal	21-26-9
Post-Grad Deg	19-14-3	Rsd: Luth	13-18-5	Rsd: Bapt	10-7-9
Den: Cath	19-10-0	35-44	16-17-7	Exec: 15-25 Yrs	10-16-8
Democrats	19-17-5	Rsd: No Rel	13-17-22	18-34	10-16-8
65+	18-11-5	Democrats	19-17-5	Coll Grad	16-15-8
Rsd: Cath	18-15-2	45-54	16-16-4	35-44	16-17-7
Neither Con/Lib	18-15-12	Emply: 11-25	17-16-7	Exec: <5 Yrs	14-15-7
Emply: 11-25	17-16-7	18-34	10-16-8	Northeast	20-14-7
Independents	16-13-10	HS or Less	16-16-11	Exec: 5-10 Yrs	14-18-7
55-64	16-13-7	Exec: 15-25 Yrs	10-16-8	Emply: 11-25	17-16-7
HS or Less	16-16-11	Neither Con/Lib	18-15-12	*Den: Non-Chr	40-20-7
35-44	16-17-7	Some Coll/Voc	13-15-3	55-64	16-13-7
Coll Grad	16-15-8	Women	15-15-6	Women	15-15-6

Question 32
Level of Involvement in Activities at Church or House of Worship (part 1*)

1. Very Involved: 27
2. Somewhat Involved: 32
3. Not Too Involved: 22
4. Not At All Involved: 20
5. No Opinion/Refused: *

* Note: Crosstabs below are for categories 1 and 2. Categories 3 and 4 are on the next page.

Very Involved		**Somewhat Involved**	
Exec: 15-25 Yrs	40-27-23-8	Den: Bapt 3	8-45-12-2
Rsd: Oth Chr	40-31-12-17	*Den: Meth	3 3-42-17-8
Den: Bapt	38-45-12-2	Some Coll/Voc	22-41-14-23
Den: Oth Chr	38-32-20-11	Emply: 250+	19-41-27-14
Rsd: Bapt	37-31-17-15	Born-Agn: Yes	34-40-18-7
*Den: Non-Chr	36-27-9-27	Rsd: Meth	18-38-26-18
*Den: Luth	35-31-27-8	Exec: 10-15 Yrs	20-38-16-26
Born-Agn: Yes	34-40-18-7	Independents	20-38-20-21
*Rsd: Non-Chr	33-33-11-22	55-64	20-36-23-21
*Den: Meth	33-42-17-8	Rsd: Pres	21-36-25-18
45-54	33-28-21-17	65+	31-35-20-15
Emply: 11-25	33-25-21-21	Exec: <5 Yrs	21-35-20-24
Den: Pres	32-29-29-11	35-44	24-34-21-20
West	32-30-17-21	Very Cons	32-34-22-13
Very Cons	32-34-22-13	Emply: 4-10	26-34-21-19
Post-Grad Deg	32-26-25-18	*Rsd: Non-Chr	33-33-11-22
65+	31-35-20-15	Northeast	23-33-20-23
HS or Less	31-24-31-13	Den: Cath	11-33-28-26
Smwt Cons	29-32-19-19	Democrats	23-33-19-25
Repblcns	29-30-24-17	Exec: 25+ Yrs	26-33-24-17

Question 32
Level of Involvement in Activities at Church or House of Worship (part 1*)

1. Very Involved: 27
2. Somewhat Involved: 32
3. Not Too Involved: 22
4. Not At All Involved: 20
5. No Opinion/Refused: *

* Note: Crosstabs below are for categories 3 and 4. Categories 1 and 2 are on the previous page.

Not Too Involved		Not at all Involved	
*Den:Ath/Agn	14-14-43-29	Den: None	8-24-18-51
HS or Less	31-24-31-13	Emply: 101-250	20-24-20-36
Rsd: Luth	26-26-29-19	*Den:Ath/Agn	14-14-43-29
Den: Pres	32-29-29-11	*Den: Non-Chr	36-27-9-27
Rsd: Cath	17-32-28-22	Exec: 10-15 Yrs	20-38-16-26
Den: Cath	11-33-28-26	Neither Con/Lib	18-33-23-26
Emply: 250+	19-41-27-14	Den: Cath	11-33-28-26
Liberal	16-30-27-26	Liberal	16-30-27-26
*Den: Luth	35-31-27-8	Democrats	23-33-19-25
Born-Agn: No	23-30-26-19	Rsd: No Rel	29-25-18-25
Rsd: Meth	18-38-26-18	18-34	26-25-25-25
Rsd: Pres	21-36-25-18	Exec: <5 Yrs	21-35-20-24
Men	27-30-25-18	Some Coll/Voc	22-41-14-23
Post-Grad Deg	32-26-25-18	Northeast	23-33-20-23
18-34	26-25-25-25	*Rsd: Non-Chr	33-33-11-22
Midwest	24-31-24-19	Exec: 5-10 Yrs	29-25-23-22
Exec: 25+ Yrs	26-33-24-17	Rsd: Cath	17-32-28-22
Coll Grad	25-30-24-21	Women	27-33-18-22
South	27-32-24-18	West	32-30-17-21
Repblcns	29-30-24-17	Emply: 11-25	33-25-21-21

Question 33
Pray Outside of Attending Religious Services? (part 1*)

1. Several Times A Day: 36
2. Once A Day: 18
3. A Few Times A Week: 18
4. Once A Week Or Less: 16
5. Never: 10
6. No Opinion/Refused: 1

* Note: Crosstabs below are for categories 1, 2, and 3. Categories 4, 5, and 6 are on the next page.

Several Times a Day		Once a Day		Few Times a Week	
Born-Agn: Yes	61-23-12	Rsd: Pres	26-29-29	*Den: Meth	22-15-41
Den: Oth Chr	54-21-8	Den: Pres	41-28-19	Rsd: Pres	26-29-29
Den: Bapt	52-23-20	Den: Cath	32-27-17	Rsd: Meth	33-10-27
Very Cons	48-23-11	Emply: 250+	29-24-22	Emply: 26-100	32-18-26
Rsd: Bapt	46-19-20	Born-Agn: No	26-23-22	*Den: Luth	36-18-25
65+	45-18-15	Very Cons	48-23-11	Born-Agn: No	26-23-22
45-54	44-19-17	Born-Agn: Yes	61-23-12	Exec: 10-15 Yrs	38-19-22
Exec: 25+ Yrs	44-16-17	Den: Bapt	52-23-20	Northeast	31-13-22
Rsd: Oth Chr	43-23-9	Rsd: Oth Chr	43-23-9	Emply: 250+	29-24-22
Women	43-18-17	South	37-21-18	35-44	33-17-21
Emply: 4-10	43-15-18	Rsd: Cath	37-21-18	Liberal	21-17-21
Post-Grad Deg	42-11-17	Independents	31-21-19	Den: Bapt	52-23-20
Den: Pres	41-28-19	Den: Oth Chr	54-21-8	*Den: Ath/Agn	8-4-20
Repblcns	40-18-18	18-34	28-21-13	Rsd: Luth	35-15-20
Smwt Cons	40-18-19	HS or Less	39-21-16	Rsd: Bapt	46-19-20
Midwest	39-17-20	Coll Grad	31-20-18	Midwest	39-17-20
HS or Less	39-21-16	Exec: 10-15 Yrs	38-19-22	Den: None	26-11-19
Some Coll/Voc	38-18-19	Emply: 101-250	26-19-16	Independents	31-21-19
Emply: 11-25	38-15-11	45-54	44-19-17	Smwt Cons	40-18-19
Exec: 10-15 Yrs	38-19-22	West	36-19-13	Exec: 15-25 Yrs	36-18-19

Question 33
Pray Outside of Attending Religious Services? (part 2*)

1. Several Times A Day: 36
2. Once A Day: 18
3. A Few Times A Week: 18
4. Once A Week Or Less: 16
5. Never: 10
6. No Opinion/Refused: 1

* Note: Crosstabs below are for categories 4, 5, and 6. Categories 1, 2, and 3 are on the previous page.

Once/Week or Less		Never		No Opinion/Refused	
Den: None	27-17-0	*Den: Ath/Agn	20-48-0	*Den: Non-Chr	27-33-7
18-34	27-12-0	*Rsd: Non-Chr	25-44-6	*Rsd: Non-Chr	25-44-6
*Den: Non-Chr	27-33-7	*Den: Non-Chr	27-33-7	*Den: Meth	15-4-4
Rsd: No Rel	26-24-0	Rsd: No Rel	26-24-0	Independents	11-15-3
*Rsd: Non-Chr	25-44-6	Emply: 101-250	19-19-0	Liberal	21-17-3
Democrats	22-13-0	Den: None	27-17-0	Neither Con/Lib	17-13-2
Exec: <5 Yrs	22-9-1	Liberal	21-17-3	Northeast	18-15-2
Liberal	21-17-3	Emply: 11-25	20-15-1	Exec: 15-25 Yrs	17-8-2
Born-Agn: No	20-7-1	Independents	11-15-3	Rsd: Meth	19-10-2
Emply: 11-25	20-15-1	Northeast	18-15-2	55-64	18-11-2
Rsd: Luth	20-10-0	West	16-15-2	West	16-15-2
*Den: Ath/Agn	20-48-0	Men	18-14-1	65+	9-11-2
Den: Cath	20-4-0	Neither Con/Lib	17-13-2	Women	15-5-1
Emply: 101-250	19-19-0	Democrats	22-13-0	Exec: <5 Yrs	22-9-1
Rsd: Meth	19-10-2	Exec: 10-15 Yrs	8-13-0	Some Coll/Voc	17-7-1
Rsd: Cath	19-5-1	Post-Grad Deg	16-13-1	Emply: 26-100	13-9-1
Exec: 5-10 Yrs	18-11-1	Coll Grad	18-12-1	Coll Grad	18-12-1
Northeast	18-15-2	Exec: 25+ Yrs	11-12-0	Born-Agn: No	20-7-1
*Den: Luth	18-4-0	18-34	27-12-0	Post-Grad Deg	16-13-1
55-64	18-11-2	Rsd: Oth Chr	12-11-1	Rsd: Oth Chr	12-11-1

Question 34 Importance of Religion in Own Life (part 1*)

1. Very Important: 57
2. Fairly Important: 26
3. Not Very Important At All: 17
4. No Opinion: 1

* Note: Crosstabs below are for categories 1 and 2. Categories 3 and 4 are on the next page.

Very Important		Fairly Important	
Born-Agn: Yes	88-10-1-0	*Den: Meth	59-41-0-0
Den: Bapt	86-14-0-0	Rsd: Meth	48-40-12-0
Den: Oth Chr	85-11-4-1	*Den: Ath/Agn	8-40-52-0
Rsd: Bapt	76-17-7-0	*Den: Non-Chr	40-33-27-0
Very Cons	74-18-7-1	Northeast	47-33-19-1
HS or Less	69-17-15-0	Born-Agn: No	57-33-10-1
Rsd: Oth Chr	68-13-16-2	Coll Grad	45-32-20-2
*Den: Luth	64-29-7-0	Rsd: Pres	56-32-12-0
Women	64-24-11-1	Liberal	39-32-28-1
65+	63-26-11-0	18-34	48-31-21-0
Midwest	63-23-14-0	Den: Pres	63-31-6-0
Den: Pres	63-31-6-0	*Rsd: Non-Chr	31-31-38-0
Smwt Cons	62-26-12-0	Rsd: No Rel	28-30-41-0
45-54	61-18-21-0	Den: Cath	57-30-13-0
Emply: 4-10	61-23-15-1	Rsd: Luth	53-30-18-0
Some Coll/Voc	61-25-15-0	Den: None	29-30-40-1
55-64	61-23-15-1	Independents	51-30-19-0
South	61-26-13-1	Emply: 101-250	45-29-26-0
Rsd: Cath	60-23-17-0	35-44	54-29-17-1
*Den: Meth	59-41-0-0	*Den: Luth	64-29-7-0

Question 34
Importance of Religion in Own Life (part 2*)

1. Very Important: 57
2. Fairly Important: 26
3. Not Very Important At All: 17
4. No Opinion: 1

* Note: Crosstabs below are for categories 3 and 4. Categories 1 and 2 are on the previous page.

Not Very Important at All		**No Opinion**	
*Den: Ath/Agn	8-40-52-0	Rsd: Oth Chr	68-13-16-2
Rsd: No Rel	28-30-41-0	Coll Grad	45-32-20-2
Den: None	29-30-40-1	Women	64-24-11-1
*Rsd: Non-Chr	31-31-38-0	Emply: 26-100	54-28-17-1
Liberal	39-32-28-1	Neither Con/Lib	50-25-24-1
*Den: Non-Chr	40-33-27-0	Northeast	47-33-19-1
Emply: 101-250	45-29-26-0	Exec: 15-25 Yrs	58-21-20-1
West	52-21-26-1	Very Cons	74-18-7-1
Neither Con/Lib	50-25-24-1	Emply: 4-10	61-23-15-1
Men	52-27-21-0	Exec: 5-10 Yrs	56-27-16-1
18-34	48-31-21-0	Den: None	29-30-40-1
45-54	61-18-21-0	Den: Oth Chr	85-11-4-1
Post-Grad Deg	56-24-20-0	55-64	61-23-15-1
Emply: 250+	56-24-20-0	35-44	54-29-17-1
Coll Grad	45-32-20-2	Liberal	39-32-28-1
Exec: 15-25 Yrs	58-21-20-1	Democrats	55-25-20-1
Democrats	55-25-20-1	West	52-21-26-1
Northeast	47-33-19-1	Exec: <5 Yrs	55-27-17-1
Independents	51-30-19-0	Born-Agn: No	57-33-10-1
Emply: 11-25	55-27-18-0	South	61-26-13-1

Question 35
Believe In God (part 1*)

1. Believe: 92
2. Not Sure: 5
3. Do Not Believe: 3
4. No Opinion: 1

*Note: Crosstabs below are for categories 1 and 2. Categories 3 and 4 are on the next page.

Believe

Den: Pres	**-0-0-0
*Den: Meth	**-0-0-0
Very Cons	**-0-0-0
Born-Agn: Yes	**-0-0-0
Den: Bapt	98-0-0-2
Rsd: Bapt	97-1-1-0
Den: Oth Chr	97-3-0-0
Rsd: Pres	97-0-3-0
Rsd: Cath	97-3-0-0
Emply: 101-250	97-0-3-0
Den: Cath	97-2-1-0
*Den: Luth	96-4-0-0
Born-Agn: No	96-4-0-1
45-54	95-3-3-0
Women	95-4-1-0
Exec: 25+ Yrs	94-5-1-0
South	94-4-1-1
Exec: 15-25 Yrs	94-4-1-1
Emply: 4-10	94-4-2-0
Some Coll/Voc	93-4-3-0

Not Sure

*Den: Ath/Agn	40-36-24-0
Rsd: No Rel	74-17-7-2
Liberal	85-9-4-2
Exec: 10-15 Yrs	90-8-0-1
West	87-8-5-0
Emply: 250+	92-8-0-0
Neither Con/Lib	87-7-6-0
Coll Grad	90-7-2-1
18-34	87-7-6-0
Independents	88-7-4-1
Den: None	88-7-6-0
*Den: Non-Chr	87-7-7-0
Emply: 26-100	88-7-4-1
*Rsd: Non-Chr	81-6-13-0
Rsd: Oth Chr	91-6-3-0
65+	91-6-2-2
Men	89-6-4-1
Exec: 5-10 Yrs	88-6-5-1
Emply: 11-25	87-6-6-2
Post-Grad Deg	89-6-3-2

Question 35
Believe In God (part 2*)

1. Believe: 92
2. Not Sure: 5
3. Do Not Believe: 3
4. No Opinion: 1

*Note: Crosstabs below are for categories 3 and 4. Categories 1 and 2 are on the previous page.

Do Not Believe

*Den: Ath/Agn	40-36-24-0
*Rsd: Non-Chr	81-6-13-0
*Den: Non-Chr	87-7-7-0
Rsd: No Rel	74-17-7-2
Neither Con/Lib	87-7-6-0
18-34	87-7-6-0
Rsd: Meth	88-4-6-2
Den: None	88-7-6-0
Emply: 11-25	87-6-6-2
West	87-8-5-0
Exec: 5-10 Yrs	88-6-5-1
Exec: <5 Yrs	91-3-5-1
Northeast	90-3-5-2
Democrats	91-3-4-1
Liberal	85-9-4-2
Men	89-6-4-1
Emply: 26-100	88-7-4-1
HS or Less	92-3-4-1
Independents	88-7-4-1
Post-Grad Deg	89-6-3-2

No Opinion

Den: Bapt	98-0-0-2
Post-Grad Deg	89-6-3-2
Northeast	90-3-5-2
Rsd: No Rel	74-17-7-2
Emply: 11-25	87-6-6-2
Rsd: Meth	88-4-6-2
35-44	90-5-3-2
Liberal	85-9-4-2
65+	91-6-2-2
Exec: 10-15 Yrs	90-8-0-1
Emply: 26-100	88-7-4-1
South	94-4-1-1
Smwt Cons	93-4-2-1
Exec: 15-25 Yrs	94-4-1-1
Men	89-6-4-1
HS or Less	92-3-4-1
Exec: 5-10 Yrs	88-6-5-1
Independents	88-7-4-1
Democrats	91-3-4-1
Aggregate	91-5-3-1

Question 36
Believe In the Devil? (part 1*)

1. Believe: 69
2. Not Sure: 11
3. Do Not Believe: 19
4. No Opinion: 1

*Note: Crosstabs below are for categories 1 and 2. Categories 3 and 4 are on the next page.

Believe		**Not Sure**	
Den: Bapt	91-5-2-2	Den: None	57-20-23-0
Born-Agn: Yes	90-3-6-1	Post-Grad Deg	56-17-26-1
Rsd: Bapt	89-6-4-1	Neither Con/Lib	54-17-30-0
Very Cons	85-6-9-0	Emply: 101-250	55-16-29-0
Den: Oth Chr	84-4-13-0	Rsd: Cath	71-16-13-0
*Den: Luth	82-11-7-0	Exec: 10-15 Yrs	71-15-13-1
Some Coll/Voc	77-9-13-1	Rsd: Luth	68-15-18-0
Repblcns	76-11-12-0	Northeast	60-15-24-1
18-34	76-8-16-0	Den: Cath	72-14-13-0
Smwt Cons	75-10-13-2	Emply: 250+	67-14-19-0
45-54	74-13-13-0	Born-Agn: No	70-13-17-1
HS or Less	74-9-17-1	45-54	74-13-13-0
Rsd: Pres	74-9-18-0	Men	69-13-17-1
Midwest	73-12-14-1	Emply: 11-25	65-13-21-1
Emply: 4-10	73-9-17-0	35-44	63-12-22-3
55-64	73-12-15-0	55-64	73-12-15-0
Den: Cath	72-14-13-0	Midwest	73-12-14-1
Rsd: Oth Chr	72-8-20-0	*Den: Ath/Agn	32-12-56-0
Den: Pres	72-9-16-3	Liberal	60-12-27-1
Rsd: Cath	71-16-13-0	Emply: 26-100	68-12-17-3

Question 36
Believe In the Devil? (part 2*)

1. Believe: 69
2. Not Sure: 11
3. Do Not Believe: 19
4. No Opinion: 1

*Note: Crosstabs below are for categories 3 and 4. Categories 1 and 2 are on the next page.

Do Not Believe	
*Rsd: Non-Chr	25-0-75-0
*Den: Non-Chr	27-0-73-0
*Den: Ath/Agn	32-12-56-0
65+	58-9-32-0
Rsd: No Rel	57-11-30-2
Neither Con/Lib	54-17-30-0
Emply: 101-250	55-16-29-0
Liberal	60-12-27-1
Post-Grad Deg	56-17-26-1
Rsd: Meth	62-12-25-2
West	68-8-24-0
Democrats	65-10-24-1
Northeast	60-15-24-1
Independents	65-11-23-1
Den: None	57-20-23-0
*Den: Meth	67-11-22-0
35-44	63-12-22-3
Exec: 5-10 Yrs	66-12-21-1
Women	69-9-21-1
Emply: 11-25	65-13-21-1

No Opinion	
Den: Pres	72-9-16-3
Emply: 26-100	68-12-17-3
35-44	63-12-22-3
Den: Bapt	91-5-2-2
Rsd: No Rel	57-11-30-2
Rsd: Meth	62-12-25-2
Smwt Cons	75-10-13-2
Rsd: Bapt	89-6-4-1
Exec: 10-15 Yrs	71-15-13-1
South	71-11-17-1
Post-Grad Deg	56-17-26-1
Northeast	60-15-24-1
Exec: 15-25 Yrs	71-10-18-1
HS or Less	74-9-17-1
Exec: 5-10 Yrs	66-12-21-1
Independents	65-11-23-1
Emply: 11-25	65-13-21-1
Women	69-9-21-1
Liberal	60-12-27-1
Democrats	65-10-24-1

Question 37
Believe In Heaven? (part 1*)

1. Believe: 84
2. Not Sure: 8
3. Do Not Believe: 7
4. No Opinion: 0

*Note: Crosstabs below are for categories 1 and 2. Categories 3 and 4 are on the next page.

Believe

Born-Agn: Yes	99-1-0-0
Den: Bapt	98-2-0-0
Very Cons	97-1-2-0
*Den: Luth	96-4-0-0
Den: Pres	94-6-0-0
Den: Oth Chr	93-3-4-0
*Den: Meth	93-7-0-0
Rsd: Bapt	91-6-3-0
Rsd: Pres	91-6-3-0
Rsd: Luth	90-3-8-0
HS or Less	89-7-4-0
Women	89-5-5-0
Den: Cath	89-8-3-0
Exec: 15-25 Yrs	89-7-4-0
South	88-6-6-0
Born-Agn: No	88-9-3-0
Emply: 4-10	88-6-6-0
Some Coll/Voc	87-5-7-0
Midwest	87-8-5-0
Rsd: Cath	87-9-4-0

Not Sure

*Den: Ath/Agn	24-36-40-0
Emply: 26-100	76-16-7-1
Rsd: No Rel	74-15-11-0
Northeast	77-14-8-1
Liberal	76-13-10-1
Post-Grad Deg	77-13-10-0
*Rsd: Non-Chr	63-13-25-0
65+	78-12-9-0
Den: None	76-12-13-0
Repblcns	86-11-3-0
Men	80-11-9-0
Coll Grad	81-10-8-1
Emply: 11-25	81-10-10-0
Exec: <5 Yrs	82-10-8-1
West	79-9-11-0
Rsd: Cath	87-9-4-0
Smwt Cons	87-9-4-0
Emply: 250+	86-9-5-0
35-44	84-9-7-0
Born-Agn: No	88-9-3-0

Question 37
Believe In Heaven? (part 2*)

1. Believe: 84
2. Not Sure: 8
3. Do Not Believe: 7
4. No Opinion: 0

*Note: Crosstabs below are for categories 3 and 4. Categories 1 and 2 are on the previous page.

Do Not Believe		No Opinion	
*Den: Ath/Agn	24-36-40-0	Emply: 26-100	76-16-7-1
*Rsd: Non-Chr	63-13-25-0	Northeast	77-14-8-1
*Den: Non-Chr	73-7-20-0	Liberal	76-13-10-1
Neither Con/Lib	75-7-18-0	Exec: <5 Yrs	82-10-8-1
Emply: 101-250	81-3-16-0	Coll Grad	81-10-8-1
Den: None	76-12-13-0	Women	89-5-5-0
West	79-9-11-0	Aggregate	84-8-7-0
Rsd: No Rel	74-15-11-0	Emply: 250+	86-9-5-0
Independents	83-7-11-0	Emply: 4-10	88-6-6-0
Rsd: Oth Chr	84-6-10-0	Exec: 15-25 Yrs	89-7-4-0
Liberal	76-13-10-1	Emply: 101-250	81-3-16-0
Democrats	83-7-10-0	Born-Agn: Yes	99-1-0-0
Post-Grad Deg	77-13-10-0	Born-Agn: No	88-9-3-0
Exec: 5-10 Yrs	83-7-10-0	Repblcns	86-11-3-0
Emply: 11-25	81-10-10-0	Exec: 5-10 Yrs	83-7-10-0
Rsd: Meth	83-8-10-0	Exec: 10-15 Yrs	85-8-7-0
18-34	83-8-9-0	Men	80-11-9-0
65+	78-12-9-0	Emply: 11-25	81-10-10-0
Men	80-11-9-0	West	79-9-11-0
Exec: 25+ Yrs	83-9-9-0	Midwest	87-8-5-0

Question 38
Believe In Hell? (part 1*)

1. Believe: 71
2. Not Sure: 11
3. Do Not Believe: 17
4. No Opinion: *

*Note: Crosstabs below are for categories 1 and 2. Categories 3 and 4 are on the next page.

Believe		**Not Sure**	
Born-Agn: Yes	96-1-3-0	*Den: Ath/Agn	24-28-48-0
Den: Bapt	93-2-2-2	Den: None	56-18-23-3
*Den: Luth	89-11-0-0	Northeast	59-17-22-2
Very Cons	89-6-5-0	Rsd: Cath	71-16-11-2
Rsd: Bapt	89-7-4-0	Rsd: Meth	63-15-19-2
Den: Oth Chr	84-5-12-0	Liberal	59-15-26-1
Some Coll/Voc	78-10-12-0	Emply: 26-100	66-14-18-1
Den: Pres	78-9-13-0	Exec: <5 Yrs	68-14-16-1
Rsd: Luth	78-13-10-0	Post-Grad Deg	60-14-24-2
Repblcns	77-12-10-0	Born-Agn: No	70-14-15-1
Midwest	77-11-11-1	Den: Cath	74-13-12-0
Rsd: Pres	76-9-15-0	55-64	70-13-15-2
Smwt Cons	76-11-12-2	Rsd: No Rel	54-13-33-0
HS or Less	75-10-14-1	Emply: 250+	72-13-13-3
Rsd: Oth Chr	75-5-19-1	Rsd: Luth	78-13-10-0
Den: Cath	74-13-12-0	Exec: 10-15 Yrs	69-13-17-1
18-34	74-10-15-0	Men	70-12-17-1
65+	74-9-17-0	Repblcns	77-12-10-0
Exec: 25+ Yrs	73-9-17-1	Coll Grad	68-12-19-1
Exec: 15-25 Yrs	73-11-16-0	35-44	69-12-17-2

Question 38
Believe In Hell? (part 2*)

1. Believe: 71
2. Not Sure: 11
3. Do Not Believe: 17
4. No Opinion: *

*Note: Crosstabs below are for categories 3 and 4. Categories 1 and 2 are on the previous page.

Do Not Believe		**No Opinion**	
*Rsd: Non-Chr	31-0-69-0	Independents	70-10-17-3
*Den: Non-Chr	40-0-60-0	Den: None	56-18-23-3
*Den: Ath/Agn	24-28-48-0	Emply: 250+	72-13-13-3
Rsd: No Rel	54-13-33-0	Northeast	59-17-22-2
Neither Con/Lib	58-11-30-1	Den: Bapt	93-2-2-2
Liberal	59-15-26-1	Post-Grad Deg	60-14-24-2
Democrats	65-10-24-1	Rsd: Meth	63-15-19-2
Post-Grad Deg	60-14-24-2	55-64	70-13-15-2
West	70-7-23-0	35-44	69-12-17-2
Den: None	56-18-23-3	Smwt Cons	76-11-12-2
Emply: 101-250	68-10-23-0	Rsd: Cath	71-16-11-2
Emply: 11-25	68-10-22-0	Women	72-9-17-1
Northeast	59-17-22-2	Exec: 10-15 Yrs	69-13-17-1
Exec: 5-10 Yrs	72-8-19-1	Exec: <5 Yrs	68-14-16-1
Rsd: Meth	63-15-19-2	Emply: 26-100	66-14-18-1
Coll Grad	68-12-19-1	Coll Grad	68-12-19-1
Rsd: Oth Chr	75-5-19-1	South	72-12-15-1
*Den: Meth	70-11-19-0	Exec: 25+ Yrs	73-9-17-1
Emply: 26-100	66-14-18-1	Neither Con/Lib	58-11-30-1
35-44	69-12-17-2	Rsd: Oth Chr	75-5-19-1

Question 39
Believe In: Miracles? (part 1*)

1. Believe: 81
2. Not Sure: 10
3. Do Not Believe: 9
4. No Opinion: 0

*Note: Crosstabs below are for categories 1 and 2. Categories 3 and 4 are on the next page.

Believe		**Not Sure**	
Den: Bapt	98-2-0-0	*Den: Luth	82-18-0-0
Born-Agn: Yes	96-3-1-0	Rsd: Pres	82-18-0-0
Women	91-5-3-0	Den: None	70-16-13-1
45-54	90-9-1-0	Den: Pres	84-16-0-0
Exec: 15-25 Yrs	90-5-5-0	Coll Grad	71-16-14-0
Den: Oth Chr	89-4-7-0	Exec: 10-15 Yrs	78-15-7-0
Rsd: Bapt	89-4-7-0	Rsd: No Rel	72-15-11-2
HS or Less	88-6-6-0	Emply: 250+	73-15-11-0
Very Cons	88-7-5-0	Liberal	72-15-13-1
Den: Cath	87-10-3-0	Independents	73-13-12-2
Smwt Cons	86-7-7-0	Neither Con/Lib	74-13-12-1
Some Coll/Voc	85-7-7-1	Men	74-13-13-0
*Den: Meth	85-7-4-4	Northeast	77-13-10-0
Rsd: Oth Chr	85-9-6-0	*Den: Ath/Agn	48-12-40-0
Den: Pres	84-16-0-0	Born-Agn: No	83-12-5-1
Emply: 4-10	84-9-6-0	35-44	77-11-12-0
Rsd: Cath	84-11-5-0	Exec: 25+ Yrs	80-11-9-0
Repblcns	83-10-7-0	Rsd: Cath	84-11-5-0
South	83-7-10-0	Midwest	81-11-8-1
Born-Agn: No	83-12-5-1	Emply: 26-100	80-11-9-0

Question 39
Believe In: Miracles? (part 2*)

1. Believe 81
2. Not Sure 10
3. Do Not Believe 9
4. No Opinion 0

*Note: Crosstabs below are for categories 3 and 4. Categories 1 and 2 are on the previous page.

Do Not Believe		No Opinion	
*Rsd: Non-Chr	50-6-44-0	*Den: Meth	85-7-4-4
*Den: Ath/Agn	48-12-40-0	18-34	80-9-8-2
*Den: Non-Chr	60-7-33-0	Rsd: No Rel	72-15-11-2
65+	71-9-20-0	Independents	73-13-12-2
Coll Grad	71-16-14-0	Rsd: Meth	75-10-13-2
Rsd: Meth	75-10-13-2	Neither Con/Lib	74-13-12-1
Men	74-13-13-0	Post-Grad Deg	82-8-9-1
Emply: 101-250	81-6-13-0	Exec: 5-10 Yrs	81-8-11-1
Liberal	72-15-13-1	Den: None	70-16-13-1
Den: None	70-16-13-1	Emply: 11-25	82-7-11-1
35-44	77-11-12-0	West	81-9-9-1
Neither Con/Lib	74-13-12-1	Liberal	72-15-13-1
Independents	73-13-12-2	Midwest	81-11-8-1
Emply: 250+	73-15-11-0	Exec: <5 Yrs	78-10-11-1
Democrats	81-8-11-0	Some Coll/Voc	85-7-7-1
Exec: <5 Yrs	78-10-11-1	Born-Agn: No	83-12-5-1
Rsd: No Rel	72-15-11-2	Emply: 4-10	84-9-6-0
Exec: 5-10 Yrs	81-8-11-1	Women	91-5-3-0
Emply: 11-25	82-7-11-1	Aggregate	81-10-9-0
Northeast	77-13-10-0	Men	74-13-13-0

Question 40
Believe In Life After Death? (part 1*)

1. Believe: 70
2. Not Sure: 17
3. Do Not Believe: 12
4. No Opinion: 1

*Note: Crosstabs below are for categories 1 and 2. Categories 3 and 4 are on the next page.

Believe		**Not Sure**	
Born-Agn: Yes	87-5-7-1	*Den: Ath/Agn	12-44-40-4
Den: Bapt	86-7-7-0	*Den: Non-Chr	47-33-20-0
Den: Pres	84-6-6-3	*Rsd: Non-Chr	31-31-38-0
Very Cons	84-10-6-0	Rsd: No Rel	54-30-13-2
Rsd: Pres	82-9-9-0	Den: None	62-25-13-0
Rsd: Bapt	80-11-7-1	Liberal	58-23-18-1
Den: Oth Chr	80-12-9-0	West	71-21-9-0
Den: Cath	79-11-9-1	Emply: 250+	68-20-11-0
*Den: Luth	79-14-7-0	Emply: 11-25	69-20-10-1
*Den: Meth	78-15-7-0	35-44	70-20-9-1
45-54	78-14-8-1	18-34	66-20-14-0
Born-Agn: No	77-14-9-1	Northeast	67-19-13-1
Exec: 10-15 Yrs	76-17-7-0	Neither Con/Lib	63-19-15-2
Smwt Cons	75-13-10-1	Exec: <5 Yrs	66-18-14-1
Rsd: Oth Chr	75-18-7-0	Post-Grad Deg	72-18-9-1
Rsd: Cath	75-12-11-2	HS or Less	71-18-12-0
Repblcns	74-14-9-2	Rsd: Oth Chr	75-18-7-0
Emply: 101-250	74-6-19-0	Exec: 5-10 Yrs	72-17-11-0
65+	74-11-14-2	Emply: 26-100	67-17-12-4
Exec: 15-25 Yrs	73-15-10-2	Men	69-17-13-1

Question 40
Believe In Life After Death? (part 2*)

1. Believe: 70
2. Not Sure: 17
3. Do Not Believe: 12
4. No Opinion: 2

*Note: Crosstabs below are for categories 3 and 4. Categories 1 and 2 are on the previous page.

Do Not Believe

*Den: Ath/Agn	12-44-40-4
*Rsd: Non-Chr	31-31-38-0
*Den: Non-Chr	47-33-20-0
Emply: 101-250	74-6-19-0
Rsd: Meth	65-15-19-0
Liberal	58-23-18-1
55-64	64-17-18-1
Exec: 25+ Yrs	67-15-16-2
Neither Con/Lib	63-19-15-2
Independents	68-16-15-0
South	71-13-15-1
18-34	66-20-14-0
65+	74-11-14-2
Exec: <5 Yrs	66-18-14-1
Democrats	69-16-14-1
Coll Grad	70-15-14-1
Den: None	62-25-13-0
Men	69-17-13-1
Rsd: No Rel	54-30-13-2
Northeast	67-19-13-1

No Opinion

*Den: Ath/Agn	12-44-40-4
Emply: 26-100	67-17-12-4
Den: Pres	84-6-6-3
Rsd: Luth	70-15-13-3
Exec: 25+ Yrs	67-15-16-2
Neither Con/Lib	63-19-15-2
Midwest	72-15-11-2
Rsd: No Rel	54-30-13-2
Exec: 15-25 Yrs	73-15-10-2
Some Coll/Voc	70-17-12-2
Women	72-16-10-2
Repblcns	74-14-9-2
65+	74-11-14-2
Rsd: Cath	75-12-11-2
Rsd: Bapt	80-11-7-1
Exec: <5 Yrs	66-18-14-1
Coll Grad	70-15-14-1
South	71-13-15-1
Aggregate	70-17-12-1
Post-Grad Deg	72-18-9-1

Question 41
Believe In Sin? (part 1*)

1. Believe: 89
2. Not Sure: 4
3. Do Not Believe: 5
4. No Opinion: 2

*Note: Crosstabs below are for categories 1 and 2. Categories 3 and 4 are on the next page.

Believe		**Not Sure**	
Den: Bapt	**-0-0-0	Emply: 26-100	87-9-1-3
Born-Agn: Yes	99-0-1-0	Northeast	80-9-7-5
Very Cons	99-0-1-0	Rsd: No Rel	83-9-4-4
Rsd: Bapt	99-0-1-0	Coll Grad	84-8-6-1
Den: Oth Chr	97-1-2-0	Neither Con/Lib	83-7-8-1
*Den: Luth	96-4-0-0	18-34	85-7-6-2
Repblcns	94-4-2-0	Rsd: Cath	89-7-3-1
Some Coll/Voc	93-3-3-1	Democrats	86-7-6-1
*Den: Non-Chr	93-0-0-7	Den: None	83-7-6-5
Exec: 10-15 Yrs	93-4-3-0	Emply: 250+	89-6-4-1
35-44	93-3-3-1	Exec: 15-25 Yrs	91-6-2-1
Women	93-2-3-1	Liberal	83-6-9-3
South	93-3-3-1	Den: Cath	92-6-2-0
*Den: Meth	93-4-4-0	Men	87-6-6-1
Rsd: Luth	93-3-3-3	45-54	91-5-3-1
Exec: 5-10 Yrs	92-3-4-1	Born-Agn: No	91-5-4-0
Den: Cath	92-6-2-0	Exec: <5 Yrs	84-5-8-3
Emply: 4-10	92-3-3-2	Aggregate	89-4-5-1
Smwt Cons	91-4-3-2	Exec: 10-15 Yrs	93-4-3-0
Born-Agn: No	91-5-4-0	*Den: Ath/Agn	64-4-32-0

Question 41
Believe In Sin? (part 2*)

1. Believe: 89
2. Not Sure: 4
3. Do Not Believe: 5
4. No Opinion: 1

*Note: Crosstabs below are for categories 3 and 4. Categories 1 and 2 are on the previous page.

Do Not Believe

*Den: Ath/Agn	64-4-32-0
*Rsd: Non-Chr	81-0-13-6
Emply: 11-25	87-3-11-0
Emply: 101-250	90-0-10-0
Independents	85-4-10-2
Rsd: Oth Chr	89-2-9-0
Liberal	83-6-9-3
Neither Con/Lib	83-7-8-1
Exec: <5 Yrs	84-5-8-3
65+	91-2-8-0
Northeast	80-9-7-5
Post-Grad Deg	91-1-7-1
Den: Pres	91-3-6-0
Men	87-6-6-1
Exec: 25+ Yrs	90-2-6-1
Democrats	86-7-6-1
West	91-3-6-1
Rsd: Pres	91-3-6-0
Coll Grad	84-8-6-1
18-34	85-7-6-2

No Opinion

*Den: Non-Chr	93-0-0-7
*Rsd: Non-Chr	81-0-13-6
Den: None	83-7-6-5
Northeast	80-9-7-5
Rsd: No Rel	83-9-4-4
Exec: <5 Yrs	84-5-8-3
Emply: 26-100	87-9-1-3
Liberal	83-6-9-3
Rsd: Luth	93-3-3-3
18-34	85-7-6-2
Emply: 4-10	92-3-3-2
HS or Less	90-3-5-2
Independents	85-4-10-2
55-64	90-4-5-2
Smwt Cons	91-4-3-2
Women	93-2-3-1
Aggregate	89-4-5-1
Men	87-6-6-1
Some Coll/Voc	93-3-3-1
Coll Grad	84-8-6-1

Question 42
Believe In Resurrection of the Dead? (part 1*)

1. Believe: 65
2. Not Sure: 15
3. Do Not Believe: 20
4. No Opinion: 1

*Note: Crosstabs below are for categories 1 and 2. Categories 3 and 4 are on the next page.

Believe		**Not Sure**	
Born-Agn: Yes	89-7-4-0	Rsd: No Rel	50-24-26-0
Den: Bapt	86-11-2-0	Den: None	50-22-28-0
Very Cons	84-9-7-0	*Den: Ath/Agn	16-20-64-0
Rsd: Bapt	77-11-11-0	Liberal	47-19-33-1
Den: Oth Chr	76-11-13-0	Exec: 25+ Yrs	65-18-17-0
*Den: Luth	75-14-11-0	Den: Cath	73-18-9-0
*Den: Meth	74-0-19-7	Rsd: Pres	56-18-26-0
Exec: 10-15 Yrs	74-17-10-0	Rsd: Cath	66-18-16-0
Den: Cath	73-18-9-0	Women	63-18-18-1
Rsd: Oth Chr	72-10-18-0	Post-Grad Deg	64-17-19-0
Smwt Cons	72-15-13-0	Exec: 10-15 Yrs	74-17-10-0
Rsd: Luth	70-10-18-3	Exec: 5-10 Yrs	61-17-22-0
Emply: 4-10	70-14-16-0	Emply: 11-25	62-16-21-1
45-54	70-12-17-1	18-34	59-16-23-1
Repblcns	70-14-15-0	Born-Agn: No	65-16-17-1
Midwest	70-16-13-2	Midwest	70-16-13-2
65+	69-15-15-0	Emply: 26-100	62-16-21-1
Den: Pres	69-13-19-0	35-44	66-16-18-0
HS or Less	69-14-18-0	Neither Con/Lib	52-15-31-1
Some Coll/Voc	68-15-16-1	Democrats	58-15-26-0

Question 42 Believe In Resurrection of the Dead? (part 2*)

1. Believe: 65
2. Not Sure: 15
3. Do Not Believe: 20
4. No Opinion: 1

*Note: Crosstabs below are for categories 3 and 4. Categories 1 and 2 are on the previous page.

Do Not Believe

*Rsd: Non-Chr	25-6-69-0
*Den: Ath/Agn	16-20-64-0
*Den: Non-Chr	40-7-53-0
Emply: 101-250	52-13-35-0
Liberal	47-19-33-1
Neither Con/Lib	52-15-31-1
Northeast	60-10-28-1
Den: None	50-22-28-0
Democrats	58-15-26-0
Rsd: Pres	56-18-26-0
Rsd: No Rel	50-24-26-0
Coll Grad	60-14-25-1
Exec: <5 Yrs	62-12-25-1
Independents	65-10-24-1
18-34	59-16-23-1
Emply: 250+	63-13-23-1
55-64	63-15-22-0
Exec: 5-10 Yrs	61-17-22-0
West	62-15-22-0
Emply: 11-25	62-16-21-1

No Opinion

*Den: Meth	74-0-19-7
Rsd: Meth	65-12-19-4
Rsd: Luth	70-10-18-3
Midwest	70-16-13-2
Exec: <5 Yrs	62-12-25-1
Emply: 26-100	62-16-21-1
Coll Grad	60-14-25-1
Emply: 250+	63-13-23-1
Born-Agn: No	65-16-17-1
Neither Con/Lib	52-15-31-1
18-34	59-16-23-1
Northeast	60-10-28-1
Exec: 15-25 Yrs	67-11-21-1
Emply: 11-25	62-16-21-1
Independents	65-10-24-1
Women	63-18-18-1
45-54	70-12-17-1
Liberal	47-19-33-1
Some Coll/Voc	68-15-16-1
Aggregate	65-15-20-1

Question 43
Believe In Good and Evil? (part 1*)

1. Believe: 96
2. Not Sure: 2
3. Do Not Believe: 1
4. No Opinion: 1

*Note: Crosstabs below are for categories 1 and 3 Categories 3 and 4 are on the next page.

Believe	
Den: Bapt	**-0-0-0
Rsd: Bapt	**-0-0-0
Post-Grad Deg	**-0-0-0
Born-Agn: Yes	99-1-0-0
Very Cons	99-1-0-0
Emply: 250+	99-1-0-0
South	98-0-1-1
Women	98-1-0-0
Exec: 25+ Yrs	98-0-2-0
Emply: 4-10	98-1-0-0
Rsd: Luth	98-3-0-0
Repblcns	97-2-0-0
35-44	97-2-0-1
Some Coll/Voc	97-1-1-1
55-64	97-1-2-0
Den: Oth Chr	97-1-1-1
65+	97-0-3-0
Exec: 15-25 Yrs	97-2-1-0
Den: Cath	97-2-1-0
*Den: Luth	96-4-0-0

Not Sure	
Northeast	93-7-0-0
Emply: 26-100	89-7-4-0
Rsd: No Rel	91-7-0-2
Den: Pres	94-6-0-0
45-54	94-6-0-0
Rsd: Pres	94-6-0-0
Coll Grad	92-5-2-1
Den: None	93-5-2-0
Neither Con/Lib	93-5-1-1
*Den: Ath/Agn	96-4-0-0
Independents	93-4-2-1
*Den: Luth	96-4-0-0
Exec: <5 Yrs	94-3-1-1
Liberal	93-3-3-1
Emply: 101-250	94-3-3-0
Men	94-3-2-1
Born-Agn: No	94-3-1-1
Rsd: Cath	95-3-2-0
HS or Less	94-3-2-1
Exec: 5-10 Yrs	95-3-1-1

Question 43
Believe In Good and Evil? (part 2*)

1. Believe: 96
2. Not Sure: 2
3. Do Not Believe: 1
4. No Opinion: 1

*Note: Crosstabs below are for categories 3 and 4. Categories 1 and 2 are on the previous page.

Do Not Believe

*Den: Non-Chr	93-0-7-0
*Rsd: Non-Chr	94-0-6-0
Emply: 26-100	89-7-4-0
18-34	93-2-3-1
Emply: 101-250	94-3-3-0
65+	97-0-3-0
Midwest	94-2-3-1
Liberal	93-3-3-1
Exec: 25+ Yrs	98-0-2-0
Men	94-3-2-1
HS or Less	94-3-2-1
Coll Grad	92-5-2-1
Independents	93-4-2-1
Emply: 11-25	94-2-2-2
Den: None	93-5-2-0
Rsd: Meth	94-2-2-2
55-64	97-1-2-0
Democrats	95-2-2-2
Smwt Cons	96-2-2-1

No Opinion

*Den: Meth	96-0-0-4
Rsd: No Rel	91-7-0-2
Emply: 11-25	94-2-2-2
Rsd: Meth	94-2-2-2
Democrats	95-2-2-2
Exec: <5 Yrs	94-3-1-1
Born-Agn: No	94-3-1-1
Neither Con/Lib	93-5-1-1
18-34	93-2-3-1
Rsd: Oth Chr	96-1-2-1
Exec: 5-10 Yrs	95-3-1-1
Den: Oth Chr	97-1-1-1
Independents	93-4-2-1
35-44	97-2-0-1
Liberal	93-3-3-1
West	96-3-1-1
Midwest	94-2-3-1
Men	94-3-2-1
Some Coll/Voc	97-1-1-1

Question 44
Experienced God's Presence/Spiritual Force? (part 1*)

1. Many Times: 40
2. Several Times: 26
3. Once Or Twice: 19
4. Never: 14
5. No Opinion: 2

*Note: Crosstabs below are for categories 1 and 2. Categories 3 and 4 are on the next page.

Many Times		Several Times	
Born-Agn: Yes	63-24-11-1	*Den: Luth	29-39-25-7
Den: Oth Chr	60-27-6-4	Rsd: Pres	47-35-15-3
Den: Pres	56-22-16-6	*Den: Meth	37-33-22-7
45-54	54-25-13-7	South	38-31-18-8
Very Cons	53-24-15-5	Democrats	36-31-20-11
Rsd: Bapt	49-27-20-3	Born-Agn: No	32-30-23-11
Rsd: Oth Chr	48-27-12-9	Rsd: Luth	30-30-20-18
Rsd: Pres	47-35-15-3	Den: Bapt	45-30-23-0
Women	46-24-18-9	Exec: 15-25 Yrs	42-29-18-9
Some Coll/Voc	46-27-16-7	Emply: 101-250	32-29-19-16
Emply: 4-10	46-26-16-9	Emply: 26-100	34-29-18-17
West	46-20-16-16	Neither Con/Lib	33-29-24-12
Den: Bapt	45-30-23-0	Some Coll/Voc	46-27-16-7
Independents	44-26-13-15	Rsd: Bapt	49-27-20-3
Exec: 10-15 Yrs	43-25-14-11	55-64	36-27-21-14
HS or Less	42-26-21-8	Men	35-27-19-17
Exec: 15-25 Yrs	42-29-18-9	Den: Oth Chr	60-27-6-4
65+	42-26-11-14	Smwt Cons	38-27-19-14
Exec: 25+ Yrs	41-24-15-18	Rsd: Oth Chr	48-27-12-9
Repblcns	41-23-20-15	Midwest	41-27-18-13

Question 44 Experienced God's Presence/Spiritual Force? (part 2*)

1. Many Times: 40
2. Several Times: 26
3. Once Or Twice: 19
4. Never: 14
5. No Opinion: 2

*Note: Crosstabs below are for categories 3 and 4. Categories 1 and 2 are on the previous page.

Once or Twice		Never	
18-34	33-22-28-17	*Den: Ath/Agn	12-16-20-52
*Den: Non-Chr	27-7-27-33	*Rsd: Non-Chr	19-6-25-44
Den: Cath	34-26-26-12	*Den: Non-Chr	27-7-27-33
*Rsd: Non-Chr	19-6-25-44	Rsd: No Rel	37-17-17-26
*Den: Luth	29-39-25-7	Northeast	33-22-23-22
Exec: 5-10 Yrs	38-25-24-12	Coll Grad	31-24-23-21
Den: None	32-22-24-21	Liberal	36-22-20-21
Neither Con/Lib	33-29-24-12	Den: None	32-22-24-21
Born-Agn: No	32-30-23-11	Emply: 250+	30-25-23-20
Rsd: Meth	33-25-23-19	Rsd: Meth	33-25-23-19
Rsd: Cath	39-24-23-12	Exec: 25+ Yrs	41-24-15-18
Emply: 250+	30-25-23-20	Post-Grad Deg	41-23-15-18
Coll Grad	31-24-23-21	Rsd: Luth	30-30-20-18
Den: Bapt	45-30-23-0	18-34	33-22-28-17
Northeast	33-22-23-22	35-44	34-26-20-17
*Den: Meth	37-33-22-7	Emply: 26-100	34-29-18-17
55-64	36-27-21-14	Men	35-27-19-17
HS or Less	42-26-21-8	Exec: <5 Yrs	38-25-19-16
Emply: 11-25	40-22-20-14	West	46-20-16-16
Rsd: Luth	30-30-20-18	Emply: 101-250	32-29-19-16

Question 45
Person Committed to Religion Will Struggle in Business World (part 1*)

1. Strongly Agree: 10
2. Somewhat Agree: 14
3. Somewhat Disagree: 21
4. Strongly Disagree: 53
5. No Opinion: 3

*Note: Crosstabs below are for categories 1 and 2. Categories 3 and 4 are on the next page.

Strongly Agree		Somewhat Agree	
HS or Less	19-14-22-43	Rsd: Luth	3-28-30-40
Very Cons	17-12-14-54	Den: Bapt	11-25-18-43
Born-Agn: Yes	16-19-15-47	Exec: 5-10 Yrs	9-20-18-50
45-54	14-16-16-50	Rsd: Bapt	6-20-21-51
Rsd: Meth	13-4-27-56	Born-Agn: Yes	16-19-15-47
Rsd: Oth Chr	13-14-12-56	*Den: Meth	4-19-26-52
*Den: Non-Chr	13-0-27-60	Democrats	11-18-21-45
South	13-17-22-46	Neither Con/Lib	8-18-20-50
*Rsd: Non-Chr	13-0-25-63	*Den: Luth	11-18-29-39
Emply: 11-25	13-13-23-47	Smwt Cons	6-17-21-55
Rsd: Pres	12-6-21-50	65+	8-17-18-51
Den: Oth Chr	12-16-14-57	South	13-17-22-46
Independents	12-9-22-55	Some Coll/Voc	11-17-18-52
Den: Bapt	11-25-18-43	45-54	14-16-16-50
35-44	11-15-23-50	Den: Oth Chr	12-16-14-57
Liberal	11-7-26-53	Rsd: Cath	8-16-15-58
Democrats	11-18-21-45	Women	9-16-21-51
Exec: 10-15 Yrs	11-8-14-60	Emply: 4-10	11-15-19-53
Exec: <5 Yrs	11-14-29-45	18-34	8-15-28-49
Rsd: No Rel	11-9-35-43	35-44	11-15-23-50

Question 45
Person Committed to Religion Will Struggle in Business World (part 2*)

1. Strongly Agree: 10
2. Somewhat Agree: 14
3. Somewhat Disagree: 21
4. Strongly Disagree: 53
5. No Opinion 3

*Note: Crosstabs below are for categories 3 and 4. Categories 1 and 2 are on the previous page.

Somewhat Disagree		Strongly Disagree	
Rsd: No Rel	11-9-35-43	55-64	7-8-19-63
Rsd: Luth	3-28-30-40	*Rsd: Non-Chr	13-0-25-63
Exec: <5 Yrs	11-14-29-45	Exec: 15-25 Yrs	9-14-15-61
*Den: Luth	11-18-29-39	Emply: 101-250	6-13-16-61
*Den: Ath/Agn	8-12-28-52	*Den: Non-Chr	13-0-27-60
18-34	8-15-28-49	Exec: 10-15 Yrs	11-8-14-60
Rsd: Meth	13-4-27-56	Coll Grad	6-12-19-58
*Den: Non-Chr	13-0-27-60	West	6-12-21-58
*Den: Meth	4-19-26-52	Born-Agn: No	4-12-25-58
Liberal	11-7-26-53	Rsd: Cath	8-16-15-58
Born-Agn: No	4-12-25-58	Northeast	9-15-17-58
Post-Grad Deg	3-14-25-57	Post-Grad Deg	3-14-25-57
*Rsd: Non-Chr	13-0-25-63	Den: Oth Chr	12-16-14-57
Den: Cath	7-12-24-57	Den: Cath	7-12-24-57
35-44	11-15-23-50	Den: Pres	9-9-16-56
Emply: 11-25	13-13-23-47	Exec: 25+ Yrs	7-10-22-56
Emply: 26-100	4-14-22-55	Rsd: Meth	13-4-27-56
Independents	12-9-22-55	Emply: 250+	9-13-22-56
South	13-17-22-46	Rsd: Oth Chr	13-14-12-56
Exec: 25+ Yrs	7-10-22-56	Repblcns	9-14-20-55

Question 46
Executive Must Do Smart Thing Despite Personal Ethics (part 1*)

1. Strongly Agree: 22
2. Somewhat Agree: 24
3. Somewhat Disagree: 14
4. Strongly Disagree: 37
5. No Opinion: 3

*Note: Crosstabs below are for categories 1 and 2. Categories 3 and 4 are on the next page.

Strongly Agree	
*Rsd: Non-Chr	44-25-13-19
*Den: Non-Chr	40-33-13-13
Rsd: Pres	38-6-24-32
18-34	31-36-13-19
65+	31-15-14-34
*Den: Luth	29-29-4-36
*Den: Ath/Agn	28-28-20-16
Emply: 11-25	28-20-13-34
Emply: 250+	28-16-15-38
HS or Less	27-24-9-35
Exec: 5-10 Yrs	26-31-16-26
Den: None	26-20-13-38
Liberal	26-30-12-31
Exec: 10-15 Yrs	25-15-10-47
Rsd: Meth	25-27-10-35
Den: Pres	25-9-22-44
Midwest	24-21-15-39
South	24-31-10-30
Men	24-22-14-37
Some Coll/Voc	24-28-15-31
Neither Con/Lib	19-29-15-35

Somewhat Agree	
*Den: Meth	22-44-11-22
18-34	31-36-13-19
*Den: Non-Chr	40-33-13-13
Democrats	23-32-14-27
South	24-31-10-30
Exec: 5-10 Yrs	26-31-16-26
Den: Cath	20-30-13-37
Liberal	26-30-12-31
Den: Bapt	14-30-9-45
Exec: <5 Yrs	20-29-14-35
Neither Con/Lib	19-29-15-35
*Den: Luth	29-29-4-36
Rsd: Bapt	16-29-16-37
Some Coll/Voc	24-28-15-31
Rsd: No Rel	22-28-9-39
*Den: Ath/Agn	28-28-20-16
35-44	17-28-17-37
Emply: 4-10	16-28-14-40
Born-Agn: No	19-27-18-35
Rsd: Meth	25-27-10-35
Smwt Cons	20-23-16-39

Question 46
Executive Must Do Smart Thing Despite Personal Ethics (part 2*)

1. Strongly Agree: 22
2. Somewhat Agree: 24
3. Somewhat Disagree: 14
4. Strongly Disagree: 37
5. No Opinion 3

*Note: Crosstabs below are for categories 3 and 4. Categories 1 and 2 are on the previous page.

Somewhat Disagree

Rsd: Pres	38-6-24-32
Den: Pres	25-9-22-44
Den: Oth Chr	14-18-21-44
*Den: Ath/Agn	28-28-20-16
Emply: 101-250	23-23-19-35
Rsd: Oth Chr	21-16-19-41
Exec: 25+ Yrs	22-18-18-37
Born-Agn: No	19-27-18-35
35-44	17-28-17-37
West	16-17-17-48
Repblcns	18-21-17-43
Coll Grad	19-27-16-38
Smwt Cons	20-23-16-39
Northeast	23-22-16-36
Post-Grad Deg	17-11-16-51
55-64	14-21-16-45
Rsd: Bapt	16-29-16-37
Exec: 5-10 Yrs	26-31-16-26
Neither Con/Lib	19-29-15-35
Some Coll/Voc	24-28-15-31

Strongly Disagree

Post-Grad Deg	17-11-16-51
Exec: 15-25 Yrs	18-18-14-48
West	16-17-17-48
45-54	22-19-11-47
Exec: 10-15 Yrs	25-15-10-47
Born-Agn: Yes	19-22-12-46
Den: Bapt	14-30-9-45
Independents	20-17-13-45
Rsd: Luth	15-25-15-45
55-64	14-21-16-45
Very Cons	21-17-14-44
Den: Oth Chr	14-18-21-44
Den: Pres	25-9-22-44
Repblcns	18-21-17-43
Rsd: Oth Chr	21-16-19-41
Emply: 4-10	16-28-14-40
Rsd: No Rel	22-28-9-39
Women	19-26-14-39
Smwt Cons	20-23-16-39
Midwest	24-21-15-39

Question 47
My Faith is Involved in Every Aspect of My Life (part 1*)

1. Strongly Agree: 47
2. Somewhat Agree: 28
3. Somewhat Disagree: 12
4. Strongly Disagree: 11
5. No Opinion: 2

*Note: Crosstabs below are for categories 1 and 2. Categories 3 and 4 are on the next page.

Strongly Agree		**Somewhat Agree**	
Born-Agn: Yes	77-21-2-0	*Den: Meth	37-56-4-4
Den: Oth Chr	71-21-5-1	Rsd: Meth	29-42-13-12
Rsd: Bapt	64-26-7-3	*Den: Luth	54-36-0-11
Den: Bapt	64-30-7-0	Emply: 250+	34-35-13-18
Very Cons	64-23-8-4	Rsd: Pres	38-35-6-18
Rsd: Oth Chr	63-21-9-6	Born-Agn: No	41-35-13-9
65+	57-18-12-8	18-34	36-35-15-14
HS or Less	57-22-10-9	South	47-34-10-7
Emply: 4-10	56-22-12-7	Rsd: Cath	42-33-17-8
Exec: 25+ Yrs	56-26-11-6	Rsd: Luth	53-33-3-13
Women	55-26-9-7	Emply: 101-250	35-32-13-13
Some Coll/Voc	54-26-12-7	Den: Cath	43-32-16-8
*Den: Luth	54-36-0-11	Exec: 5-10 Yrs	47-32-10-12
45-54	53-28-7-10	Liberal	31-32-18-19
55-64	53-24-14-8	Emply: 26-100	39-32-14-12
Den: Pres	53-31-6-9	Den: Pres	53-31-6-9
Midwest	53-27-9-10	Coll Grad	35-31-12-19
Rsd: Luth	53-33-3-13	Repblcns	47-30-14-7
Exec: 10-15 Yrs	51-25-8-8	Smwt Cons	47-30-12-8
Neither Con/Lib	51-23-12-14	35-44	38-30-15-14

Question 47
My Faith is Involved in Every Aspect of My Life (part 2*)

1. Strongly Agree: 47
2. Somewhat Agree: 28
3. Somewhat Disagree: 12
4. Strongly Disagree: 11
5. No Opinion: 2

*Note: Crosstabs below are for categories 3 and 4. Categories 1 and 2 are on the previous page.

Somewhat Disagree		Strongly Disagree	
*Den: Ath/Agn	24-4-28-40	*Rsd: Non-Chr	25-13-19-44
Den: None	28-26-25-20	*Den: Ath/Agn	24-4-28-40
Rsd: No Rel	37-13-24-20	*Den: Non-Chr	27-27-13-33
*Rsd: Non-Chr	25-13-19-44	Den: None	28-26-25-20
Post-Grad Deg	45-30-18-6	Rsd: No Rel	37-13-24-20
Liberal	31-32-18-19	Coll Grad	35-31-12-19
Rsd: Cath	42-33-17-8	Northeast	39-24-16-19
West	45-23-16-12	Liberal	31-32-18-19
Northeast	39-24-16-19	Emply: 250+	34-35-13-18
Exec: 15-25 Yrs	46-25-16-11	Rsd: Pres	38-35-6-18
Den: Cath	43-32-16-8	Independents	47-27-10-15
18-34	36-35-15-14	Democrats	49-22-12-15
35-44	38-30-15-14	Exec: <5 Yrs	40-29-14-14
Men	40-29-15-14	Neither Con/Lib	51-23-12-14
Emply: 26-100	39-32-14-12	Men	40-29-15-14
Exec: <5 Yrs	40-29-14-14	18-34	36-35-15-14
Repblcns	47-30-14-7	35-44	38-30-15-14
55-64	53-24-14-8	Emply: 101-250	35-32-13-13
Rsd: Meth	29-42-13-12	Rsd: Luth	53-33-3-13
*Den: Non-Chr	27-27-13-33	West	45-23-16-12

Question 48
We'll be Called Before God to Answer for Our Sins (part 1*)

1. Strongly Agree: 68
2. Somewhat Agree: 12
3. Somewhat Disagree: 6
4. Strongly Disagree: 9
5. No Opinion: 5

*Note: Crosstabs below are for categories 1 and 2. Categories 3 and 4 are on the next page.

Strongly Agree		Somewhat Agree	
Den: Bapt	98-0-0-0	Emply: 101-250	55-26-10-10
Born-Agn: Yes	97-3-0-0	*Den: Luth	68-25-4-0
Rsd: Bapt	91-1-3-1	*Den: Meth	74-22-4-0
Very Cons	91-4-2-2	Rsd: Pres	68-21-3-6
Den: Oth Chr	83-6-4-5	Born-Agn: No	68-20-4-3
Some Coll/Voc	79-7-4-7	Den: Pres	75-19-3-0
Den: Cath	77-16-2-2	55-64	65-19-3-8
HS or Less	76-13-2-8	Rsd: Luth	65-18-5-13
Den: Pres	75-19-3-0	Rsd: No Rel	50-17-2-24
Emply: 4-10	74-10-4-6	Neither Con/Lib	56-17-6-17
*Den: Meth	74-22-4-0	Exec: 10-15 Yrs	71-17-1-6
South	73-9-4-9	Rsd: Cath	70-16-7-2
Midwest	73-14-5-5	Northeast	61-16-8-10
Smwt Cons	73-15-4-6	Coll Grad	60-16-8-10
65+	72-2-6-9	Den: Cath	77-16-2-2
Repblcns	72-15-4-5	Den: None	51-15-10-17
Exec: 10-15 Yrs	71-17-1-6	Emply: 250+	62-15-9-9
Exec: 15-25 Yrs	71-13-7-5	Repblcns	72-15-4-5
Women	71-14-5-7	Smwt Cons	73-15-4-6
Rsd: Cath	70-16-7-2	Women	71-14-5-7

Question 48
We'll be Called Before God to Answer for Our Sins (part 2*)

1. Strongly Agree: 68
2. Somewhat Agree: 12
3. Somewhat Disagree: 6
4. Strongly Disagree: 9
5. No Opinion: 5

*Note: Crosstabs below are for categories 3 and 4. Categories 1 and 2 are on the previous page.

Somewhat Disagree

*Rsd: Non-Chr	25-6-25-31
*Den: Non-Chr	33-7-20-27
*Den: Ath/Agn	20-8-12-48
Liberal	52-12-11-15
Post-Grad Deg	53-14-10-13
Emply: 101-250	55-26-10-10
Den: None	51-15-10-17
45-54	70-10-9-7
Emply: 250+	62-15-9-9
Northeast	61-16-8-10
Coll Grad	60-16-8-10
Democrats	64-12-8-11
Independents	65-8-8-13
Exec: 15-25 Yrs	71-13-7-5
Rsd: Cath	70-16-7-2
Exec: <5 Yrs	65-14-7-12
West	62-11-7-13
Emply: 26-100	67-12-7-11
Men	66-10-7-11
Rsd: Oth Chr	70-7-6-12

Strongly Disagree

*Den: Ath/Agn	20-8-12-48
*Rsd: Non-Chr	25-6-25-31
*Den: Non-Chr	33-7-20-27
Rsd: No Rel	50-17-2-24
Den: None	51-15-10-17
Neither Con/Lib	56-17-6-17
Liberal	52-12-11-15
Emply: 11-25	64-10-6-14
Independents	65-8-8-13
West	62-11-7-13
18-34	70-13-3-13
Post-Grad Deg	53-14-10-13
Rsd: Luth	65-18-5-13
Rsd: Oth Chr	70-7-6-12
Exec: <5 Yrs	65-14-7-12
Democrats	64-12-8-11
Men	66-10-7-11
Exec: 5-10 Yrs	69-10-5-11
Emply: 26-100	67-12-7-11
Coll Grad	60-16-8-10

Question 49
Because of My Faith, I've Forgiven People Who Hurt Me Deeply (part 1*)

1. Strongly Agree: 65
2. Somewhat Agree: 19
3. Somewhat Disagree: 6
4. Strongly Disagree: 6
5. No Opinion: 4

*Note: Crosstabs below are for categories 1 and 2. Categories 3 and 4 are on the next page.

Born-Agn: Yes	83-13-1-1
Den: Bapt	82-11-5-2
Very Cons	82-13-1-3
Den: Oth Chr	77-17-1-1
Rsd: Oth Chr	76-12-2-5
45-54	73-16-5-3
Rsd: Bapt	73-17-6-3
Exec: 15-25 Yrs	72-15-5-5
Den: Pres	72-19-3-3
Women	71-18-2-4
Emply: 4-10	71-17-4-4
65+	71-11-5-11
South	70-17-6-4
Some Coll/Voc	70-18-4-5
Exec: 5-10 Yrs	68-12-9-8
Rsd: Cath	68-20-7-2
*Den: Luth	68-29-0-4
Den: Cath	68-23-4-2
Exec: 25+ Yrs	67-20-1-5
HS or Less	67-18-6-8
*Den: Meth	67-33-0-0
Emply: 250+	57-32-4-8
*Den: Luth	68-29-0-4
Rsd: Luth	58-28-5-8
Born-Agn: No	65-27-2-2
Rsd: Pres	62-26-6-3
Exec: <5 Yrs	58-25-8-7
Independents	61-25-5-7
Rsd: Meth	65-25-2-8
35-44	60-24-7-7
Exec: 10-15 Yrs	65-24-1-7
Midwest	65-23-5-5
Den: Cath	68-23-4-2
Neither Con/Lib	60-23-7-7
Coll Grad	60-22-6-6
Northeast	59-22-7-8
55-64	64-21-4-5
Liberal	53-21-11-8
Smwt Cons	67-20-4-7
Rsd: Cath	68-20-7-2

Question 49
Because of My Faith, I've Forgiven People Who Hurt Me Deeply (part 2*)

1. Strongly Agree: 65
2. Somewhat Agree: 19
3. Somewhat Disagree: 6
4. Strongly Disagree: 6
5. No Opinion 4

*Note: Crosstabs below are for categories 3 and 4. Categories 1 and 2 are on the previous page.

Somewhat Disagree

*Den: Non-Chr	53-13-13-20
*Rsd: Non-Chr	50-6-13-31
*Den: Ath/Agn	36-12-12-32
Liberal	53-21-11-8
Rsd: No Rel	50-13-11-17
Den: None	57-16-11-13
Emply: 101-250	61-16-10-10
Exec: 5-10 Yrs	68-12-9-8
Men	61-20-8-8
18-34	60-20-8-10
Emply: 26-100	63-17-8-5
Democrats	66-18-8-6
Exec: <5 Yrs	58-25-8-7
Neither Con/Lib	60-23-7-7
35-44	60-24-7-7
Rsd: Cath	68-20-7-2
Northeast	59-22-7-8
Post-Grad Deg	65-18-7-8
Emply: 11-25	62-17-7-11
Coll Grad	60-22-6-6

Strongly Disagree

*Den: Ath/Agn	36-12-12-32
*Rsd: Non-Chr	50-6-13-31
*Den: Non-Chr	53-13-13-20
Rsd: No Rel	50-13-11-17
Den: None	57-16-11-13
65+	71-11-5-11
Emply: 11-25	62-17-7-11
18-34	60-20-8-10
Emply: 101-250	61-16-10-10
West	63-16-5-9
Men	61-20-8-8
Post-Grad Deg	65-18-7-8
Northeast	59-22-7-8
HS or Less	67-18-6-8
Exec: 5-10 Yrs	68-12-9-8
Liberal	53-21-11-8
Rsd: Meth	65-25-2-8
Emply: 250+	57-32-4-8
Rsd: Luth	58-28-5-8
Neither Con/Lib	60-23-7-7

Question 50
In Last Year: Volunteered for Groups That Help People

1. Yes: 79
2. No: 21
3. Refused: 0

Yes		No		Refused	
Den: Oth Chr	88-12-0	HS or Less	67-33-0	Exec: 15-25 Yrs	86-13-1
Den: Pres	88-13-0	Den: None	70-30-0	Emply: 11-25	72-27-1
Post-Grad Deg	88-13-0	18-34	71-29-0	West	81-18-1
Born-Agn: Yes	87-13-0	Exec: <5 Yrs	71-29-0	Men	80-20-0
Rsd: Oth Chr	87-13-0	Rsd: Bapt	71-29-0	Aggregate	79-21-0
Exec: 15-25 Yrs	86-13-1	Rsd: No Rel	72-28-0	Emply: 101-250	74-26-0
45-54	85-15-0	Emply: 11-25	72-27-1	Emply: 250+	82-18-0
Rsd: Pres	85-15-0	Midwest	73-27-0	Exec: 5-10 Yrs	83-17-0
*Den: Meth	85-15-0	Democrats	74-26-0	Exec: 10-15 Yrs	76-24-0
Repblcns	85-15-0	Emply: 101-250	74-26-0	Exec: <5 Yrs	71-29-0
Coll Grad	84-16-0	*Rsd: Non-Chr	75-25-0	Exec: 25+ Yrs	80-20-0
Northeast	84-16-0	*Den: Luth	75-25-0	Born-Agn: Yes	87-13-0
Exec: 5-10 Yrs	83-17-0	Liberal	75-25-0	Born-Agn: No	78-22-0
Emply: 26-100	83-17-0	65+	75-25-0	Repblcns	85-15-0
Emply: 250+	82-18-0	*Den: Ath/Agn	76-24-0	Democrats	74-26-0
Very Cons	82-18-0	Exec: 10-15 Yrs	76-24-0	Independents	80-20-0
West	81-18-1	Den: Bapt	77-23-0	Emply: 4-10	80-20-0
Smwt Cons	81-19-0	Neither Con/Lib	77-23-0	Women	78-22-0
35-44	81-19-0	Some Coll/Voc	77-23-0	Emply: 26-100	83-17-0
Exec: 25+ Yrs	80-20-0	Women	78-22-0	Midwest	73-27-0

Question 51
In Last Year: Given Money to Charity Other Than Church?

1. Yes: 88
2. No: 11
3. Refused: 1

Yes		No		Refused	
Post-Grad Deg	97-3-0	HS or Less	74-25-1	*Den: Luth	86-11-4
*Den: Meth	96-4-0	18-34	78-22-0	Den: Pres	84-13-3
55-64	94-6-0	Rsd: Oth Chr	81-18-1	Rsd: Pres	91-6-3
Rsd: Meth	94-6-0	Very Cons	82-17-1	Emply: 11-25	88-11-2
Coll Grad	94-6-0	Emply: 26-100	84-16-0	35-44	88-10-2
*Rsd: Non-Chr	94-6-0	Den: Oth Chr	85-15-0	Exec: 10-15 Yrs	85-14-1
Den: Bapt	93-7-0	West	85-15-1	Emply: 250+	91-8-1
Smwt Cons	93-7-0	Den: None	86-14-0	Neither Con/Lib	85-14-1
Exec: 25+ Yrs	91-9-0	Neither Con/Lib	85-14-1	Northeast	89-10-1
Rsd: Pres	91-6-3	Exec: 10-15 Yrs	85-14-1	Exec: 15-25 Yrs	91-8-1
Emply: 250+	91-8-1	*Den: Non-Chr	87-13-0	Men	87-12-1
Den: Cath	91-9-0	Exec: <5 Yrs	86-13-1	Rsd: Oth Chr	81-18-1
South	91-9-0	Rsd: Bapt	87-13-0	Very Cons	82-17-1
Exec: 15-25 Yrs	91-8-1	Liberal	87-13-0	HS or Less	74-25-1
Democrats	91-9-1	Exec: 5-10 Yrs	87-13-0	Independents	90-9-1
Independents	90-9-1	Some Coll/Voc	87-13-1	Democrats	91-9-1
Emply: 101-250	90-10-0	Den: Pres	84-13-3	West	85-15-1
Rsd: Luth	90-10-0	Rsd: Cath	88-12-0	Midwest	87-12-1
Women	90-10-0	Midwest	87-12-1	Born-Agn: Yes	87-12-1
Born-Agn: No	90-10-1	Men	87-12-1	Exec: <5 Yrs	86-13-1

Question 52
In Last Year: Given Money to Your Church/Synagogue/Religion?

1. Yes: 74
2. No: 25
3. Refused: 1

Yes		No		Refused	
Born-Agn: Yes	96-4-1	Den: None	35-65-0	Den: Pres	81-16-3
Den: Bapt	93-7-0	*Den: Ath/Agn	40-60-0	Rsd: Pres	71-26-3
Den: Oth Chr	92-8-0	Rsd: No Rel	57-43-0	Northeast	76-22-2
*Den: Luth	89-11-0	Liberal	58-41-1	Emply: 11-25	73-25-2
*Den: Meth	89-11-0	West	63-36-1	Exec: <5 Yrs	72-27-1
Den: Cath	89-11-0	Neither Con/Lib	67-33-0	Emply: 26-100	71-28-1
Very Cons	85-14-1	18-34	67-33-0	Exec: 15-25 Yrs	75-24-1
Born-Agn: No	85-15-0	Emply: 101-250	68-32-0	Very Cons	85-14-1
65+	83-17-0	*Rsd: Non-Chr	69-31-0	HS or Less	70-29-1
Smwt Cons	82-18-0	35-44	69-30-1	35-44	69-30-1
Den: Pres	81-16-3	HS or Less	70-29-1	Liberal	58-41-1
Post-Grad Deg	81-19-0	Women	71-29-0	Democrats	71-28-1
Exec: 25+ Yrs	80-20-0	Democrats	71-28-1	West	63-36-1
55-64	80-20-0	Exec: 10-15 Yrs	72-28-0	Born-Agn: Yes	96-4-1
Midwest	80-20-0	Emply: 26-100	71-28-1	Men	77-22-1
Repblcns	79-21-0	Independents	73-27-0	Coll Grad	73-26-1
Rsd: Cath	79-21-0	Rsd: Meth	73-27-0	Aggregate	74-25-1
Rsd: Oth Chr	78-22-0	45-54	73-27-0	Women	71-29-0
Rsd: Bapt	77-23-0	Exec: <5 Yrs	72-27-1	Repblcns	79-21-0
Men	77-22-1	*Den: Non-Chr	73-27-0	Emply: 4-10	75-25-0

Question 55
Describe Yourself as a Born-Again or Evangelical Christian?

1. Yes: 43
2. No: 51
3. Refused: 6

Yes		**No**		**Refused**	
Born-Agn: Yes	**-0-0	Born-Agn: No	0-**-0	Rsd: Pres	26-59-15
Rsd: Bapt	83-15-2	*Den: Meth	11-85-4	Den: Pres	41-47-13
Den: Bapt	82-16-2	Liberal	15-82-4	Rsd: Luth	44-44-12
Very Cons	63-31-7	Den: Cath	22-76-2	Northeast	25-64-11
65+	61-34-5	Rsd: Cath	24-73-3	18-34	47-42-11
Rsd: No Rel	58-32-11	Emply: 101-250	29-71-0	*Den: Luth	32-57-11
Den: Oth Chr	57-35-8	Post-Grad Deg	24-67-9	Rsd: No Rel	58-32-11
HS or Less	56-34-10	Rsd: Meth	32-65-3	HS or Less	56-34-10
South	55-40-5	Northeast	25-64-11	Exec: <5 Yrs	45-45-10
Some Coll/Voc	55-40-5	Coll Grad	34-63-3	Post-Grad Deg	24-67-9
Emply: 4-10	50-45-5	Emply: 26-100	32-62-6	Den: Oth Chr	57-35-8
Repblcns	49-46-5	Independents	33-60-7	Rsd: Oth Chr	44-48-8
Neither Con/Lib	48-48-4	Rsd: Pres	26-59-15	Smwt Cons	42-51-7
18-34	47-42-11	35-44	37-58-5	Emply: 250+	39-54-7
Exec: <5 Yrs	45-45-10	Midwest	39-57-3	West	43-50-7
Exec: 25+ Yrs	45-51-4	*Den: Luth	32-57-11	Independents	33-60-7
Exec: 10-15 Yrs	45-51-4	Exec: 15-25 Yrs	38-57-5	Very Cons	63-31-7
Women	45-50-6	45-54	39-56-6	Men	41-53-6
Emply: 11-25	44-51-5	Exec: 5-10 Yrs	41-55-5	Aggregate	43-51-6
Rsd: Oth Chr	44-48-8	Democrats	41-54-4	Emply: 26-100	32-62-6